Power To The People

Power To The People

Johan Norberg

Power To The People
Copyright © 2015 Free To Choose Network
FIRST EDITION
Sumner Books
737 3rd St
Hermosa Beach, California 90254
1-310-337-7003
ISBN 978-1-939104-12-0
CREATORS PUBLISHING

CONTENTS

~ ~ ~

Introduction

The world is improving. Low- and middle income-countries are making rapid progress and poverty is being reduced faster than at any other point in history. Two hundred twenty people rise out of poverty every minute. But this also means that the thirst for energy in developing countries is growing by the day. People there see how we in the west live and refuse to be left behind. This presents the world with an incredible challenge.

What happens to the planet if everybody wants to consume and travel the way we in the west do? Will the energy resources be sufficient for us all? How are we going to maintain our standard of living? And how will we get power to all the people?

These were the questions in my mind when I was asked to write and present a documentary on energy for Free To Choose Media, to be aired on PBS in January 2015.

I am not an energy expert, so for me this became a journey of exploration. I read about these issues and sought out the experts and asked them about their thoughts. I traveled to huge solar plants in the Saharan desert and to a gigantic hydropower plant on the Columbia River, to a hydraulic fracking site in Pennsylvania and to an off-grid community in Oregon. I have looked at the large-scale energy transition in Germany with all its unintended consequences, and at trucking companies that are putting natural gas into its trucks. And I have talked to farmers, scientists, environmentalists and Moroccans about what life is like without access to electricity.

I saw huge problems. Every energy source had problems and limitations, making it difficult to be a cheerleader for any of them. But, I also saw experiments and innovation and an accumulation of knowledge on a huge scale, which gave me hope for the future. Especially if we are aware of the trade-offs involved and are a bit humble about the scale of the challenge. Especially if governments step back from top-down imposed solutions that put all our eggs into one basket.

In the debate, we mostly hear extreme positions: some shout "Drill baby, drill!" while others claim that no energy source is good enough, and that we are poisoning the planet whatever we do. Some people are in love with a particular energy source, and others hate it and cheer on something else. Governments pick energy sources that they like or that happen to have the best lobbyists.

It seems difficult to have a balanced discussion about the choices we are facing. But we need one, if we are serious about giving people around the world opportunities *and* saving the planet. We will need more energy in the future to power the next steps mankind will take and to make sure that everyone around the world gets the chance for a good life, free from poverty.

In the first chapter I explain what is at stake, especially for the world's poor. In the second chapter I look at the different energy sources that are available, their costs and benefits. In the third chapter I look at the problem of top-down planning in the energy sector and in the fourth chapter I explore the alternative. In the concluding fifth chapter I try to summarize what I learned, what I think it all says about our future and the prospects for solving the energy problem.

I would like to thank everybody who helped make the research and the filming of the show possible the power plants on three continents that welcomed us, everybody we interviewed and all those who opened up their homes and workplaces to the film crew.

I would also like to thank the executive producers of the film, Bob Chitester and Tom Skinner, producer Barbara Potter and director Jim Taylor. Jim also assisted me greatly in writing the script, and therefore helped me to develop many of my thoughts on this subject. I also owe a debt of gratitude to Daniel B. Botkin who provided us with many ideas and valuable research. His book *Powering the Future: A Scientists Guide to Energy Independence* is an excellent next read if this book makes you interested in energy questions.

Mattias Bengtsson gave me important help with both ideas and data for the film and the book. I have also benefited greatly from talking to Anders Ydstedt, Nicklas Skår and Tobias Wahlqvist about these subjects.

Johan Norberg

Malmö, November 2014

1. Empowerment

"There is no substitute for energy. The whole edifice of modern society is built on energy. It is not 'just another commodity' but the precondition of all commodities, a basic factor equal with air, water, and earth."

E.F. Schumacher

You just flick a switch and suddenly there is light. You press a button and music fills the room, your food is prepared, a machine washes your clothes. On a cool day it warms your house, on a warm day, it keeps you cool. To someone who has never experienced electricity before, it must seem like magic. An invisible force brought to you from miles and miles away through a slender wire. And it can do almost anything.

When you need to go somewhere or buy a product from other places, you rely on different forms of fuel to provide the propulsion. Without reflecting on it, almost every single thing you do every day is dependent on modern sources of energy. We take it for granted. It's everywhere.

All life needs energy. For most life as we know it, the amount of energy needed to continue living is a given. If you do not get enough energy through heat and nourishment you die. Regardless of whether you are a singular living cell, a plant or an animal, you really do not have the ability to use more energy than you need to stay alive.

Once the world was like that for us humans as well – and it is still the case for too many people. Almost everything that had to be done, had to be done by human labor or animals, controlled and directed by men. The word "manufacturing" derives from the Latin words *manu* (hand) and *facere* (to perform). It was something that humans had to do by hand.

Over a fairly short time – just a few thousand years – man has, step-by-step, found new ways of using external energy supplies and use that energy for his own benefit. First slowly and then during the last couple of hundred years, more and more rapidly through an energy revolution that has totally transformed the world and the way we live.

The enormous increase in our use of energy has been a requirement for raising our standard of living. It has lengthened our lives and made it possible to fill our longer lives with more than the daily toil to keep us alive; it has made it possible to give our lives fulfillment.

"Thank you power station"

Modern life has been powered by our increasing ability to harness and put energy to use. It has made it possible to increase agricultural production to a sustainable level thanks to artificial fertilizers, pesticides, irrigation and farm machines that run on diesel. Refrigeration and petroleum-based plastic has reduced waste in the food sector and modern transport systems have made it possible to get food from places with a surplus into areas with deficits. These innovations have set mankind free from the whims of nature and the weather which previously resulted in crop failures and hunger. Before the modern era, life expectancy in the west was around 20-30 years. Now it is close to 80 years.

As this technology spread to poorer parts of the world, global hunger was drastically reduced. Sixty years ago, around half of the world's population lived in chronic undernourishment. Today around eleven percent does, according to the UN's Food and Agricultural Organization.

Modern energy sources make it possible to extract and refine modern materials and to run equipment, power tools and industrial machinery so that people's labor has become less strenuous. Modern energy fuels the ships, trains, trucks and planes that transport goods to our supermarkets and us to our destinations. Modern energy sources made it possible to produce and run home appliances and hospitals. They gave us paper and print for newspapers, and made radio, television, the internet and cell phones possible. At a flick of a switch we expect electricity to light our homes or gas to stream out of pumps to power our cars.

The historian Tony Wrigley argued that new forms of energy was the reason why the industrial revolution succeeded in Britain, and saved its population from the Malthusian trap of growth resulting in more mouths to feed, income stagnation and more deaths. An organic economy that grew its own fuel would not have been able to break

4

the cycle, but when the British started mining coal they got an extra power supply that made them more productive in all areas. The British forests were disappearing rapidly, as they needed wood for fuel and construction, so they began to use coal in steam engines to convert heat to mechanical energy. This was an amazing breakthrough.

Wrigley estimates that if England and Wales had replaced all its coal with wood in 1850, it would have had to harvest 150 percent of all the land. The capacity of the British steam engines by 1870 was equivalent to the manual labor of forty million men. That many men would have had to consume some 320 million bushels of wheat a year – more than three times the entire wheat harvest. Had they relied only on renewable sources - like trees - our ancestors would have been stuck. Coal made it possible for the British to lift themselves up by their own bootstraps. [i]

Compared to our forefathers, we in the developed world live in a time of abundant energy. We take the accessibility of energy for granted – it's almost seen as a right. The British writer Matt Ridley points out that external energy supplies have turned us all into kings, because we can now control a power equivalent to hundreds of men. For the first time, each and every one of us can now control much more energy than we can produce ourselves:

> *"Since a reasonably fit person on an exercise bicycle can generate about fifty watts, this means that it would take 150 slaves, working eight-hour shifts each, to pedal you to your current lifestyle. (Americans would need 600 slaves, French 360 and Nigerians 16.) Next time you lament human dependence on fossil fuels, pause to imagine that for every family of four you see in the street, there should be 600 unpaid slaves back home, living in abject poverty: if they had any better lifestyle they would need their own slaves. That is close to a trillion people."* [ii]

The idea that energy is an indispensable tool for humans who seek self-realization and happiness might sound too materialistic for some. But just think about the liberating force of such a fairly simple household appliance as the washing machine. That is what my countryman Hans Rosling did. Rosling is a Professor of International

5

Health and the founder of the Gapminder Foundation that promotes global development.

In a TED-talk given in 2010, Rosling tells the story of when he was four years old and saw his mother load a washing machine for the very first time in her life:

"That was a great day for my mother. My mother and father had been saving money for years to be able to buy that machine, and the first day it was going to be used; even Grandma was invited to see the machine. And Grandma was even more excited. Throughout her life she had been heating water with firewood, and she had hand washed laundry for seven children. And now she was going to watch electricity do that work."

For Rosling's grandmother the washing machine itself might be like magic. But as Rosling notices, the real magic is not the washing machine but what it makes possible:

"My mother explained the magic with this machine. She said, 'Now Hans, we have loaded the laundry. The machine will make the work. And now we can go to the library.' Because this is the magic: you load the laundry, and what do you get out of the machine? You get books out of the machines, children's books. And mother got time to read for me.

And she also got books for herself. She managed to study English and learn that as a foreign language. And she read so many novels, so many different novels.

And what we said, my mother and me: 'Thank you industrialization. Thank you steel mill. Thank you power station. And thank you chemical processing industry that gave us time to read books'." [iii]

And all of that because of power to the people.

A hundred years ago, the average American household spent almost 60 hours a week cooking, cleaning and washing clothes. Electrical stoves, microwaves, vacuum cleaners, hot and cold running water, dishwashers and washing machines have given us, especially women, the time to study and work outside the home. In a sense, abundant

6

energy has enabled women to join the working world, to excel and succeed where they hadn't before.

If we understand how essential energy abundance has been to save lives and liberate us in the rich world, we must also realize that the biggest problem in our world today is a lack of cheap energy in poor countries, where people aspire to a better and richer life, just like Rosling's mother did.

A Tale of Two Villages

Power is coming to the developing world. I travelled to Morocco to see for myself. Morocco is a country in western North Africa with a population of over 33 million and an area the size of California. For the last two decades economic growth has been steady and is now estimated at around four to five percent per year.

Energy use is, of course, much lower than in the US – one thirteenth per capita. But it's growing and forecasts indicate that energy consumption will rise six percent per year between 2012 and 2050. That might not sound like much, but it means that the middle of this century, a Moroccan would consume as much energy as today's American.

When I visited a bustling market - a medina - in Morocco it was certainly far from your average American super market in its use of energy. Still, I could see modern sources of energy being used in almost every form. Bottled gas fires the stoves for the street vendor and electrical energy powers the lights. Electricity also powers the scales and the all- important credit card readers. It drives small manufacturing tools and automated weaving machines. TV's and computers abound.

For many Moroccans, however, energy is not as easy to come by as it is in the medina, even though it's a matter of life and death.

Stretching 1,500 miles through Algeria, Tunisia and Morocco, the Atlas Mountains separate the Atlantic coastline of Morocco from the dry and harsh climate of the Sahara Desert. The small villages on the Saharan side are mostly Berber. Their residents are descendants of the pre-Arab inhabitants of North Africa. After a few hours on bumpy dirt roads you find the tiny village of Issidan Izdar. Its villagers live today much like they did hundreds of years ago.

I paid a visit to Hamma Ait M'Rim and his extended family. He is 66 years old and six of his children, with their children, live in his home. They have built their stone homestead a short walk up the hill from their neighbors. All of the family members contribute to the family's wellbeing and survival.

Hamma tends the goats and sheep. They feed on grains, seeds and dry grasses. Every day Hamma's wife, Rkia, pounds and grinds the pits of dried dates so that the farm animals can easily digest them.

Cousins Zahra and Fatima weave traditional wool rugs for sale in the local marketplace. These generate the cash needed to buy food and supplies for the family. The Berbers are well known for their colorful, handmade carpets. Cousin Mouhamed rides to the well and brings jugs of water back each day for drinking, cooking and washing.

Safia, the eldest sister, walks miles through the desert each day to collect firewood for cooking. There aren't any trees in this part of the Sahara, so she picks up dry bushes and brush. This biomass is essential fuel for the family, but this kind of collecting is also contributing to the de-vegetation and expansion of the Sahara.

The author in Issidan Izdar, Morocco, a village without power

The women of the family all take part in the preparation of meals from grinding wheat, to sifting flour for bread making. Their food is kept in a stone room, which maintains a cool temperature throughout the day. Meat and grains are stored high up, near the rafters. A weekly trip to the market supplies the family with vegetables. Twice daily, Aunt Fatima cooks bread - a diet staple - in a cast iron pan over an open flame.

As I joined the men for lunch – women and men eat in separate rooms as is the custom when there are visitors – Hamma's son Elhoussaine, who was home from college, and other men from the village were eager to catch up on what is happening in the surrounding villages.

Keltouma, Hamma and Rkia's ten-year-old daughter, attends school every day with her cousin, Hassan. They walk a short distance from the village to the one room schoolhouse. The children in this classroom range in age from six to 13 years old. Their teacher, Mouad, shares the job with one other teacher. There are 11 boys and four girls. If they're lucky, some of them might go on to high school or college. School is dismissed late in the day and the children walk together back to their houses, up on the hill.

The Ait M'Rim family lives a good life. They have food, clothing, shelter and a means of earning money. But when the sun sets and the animals are safely tucked away in the courtyard there is something no one in their village has - electricity.

You might think that for people like Hamma and his family Moroccan village life is simple and pure, close to nature, far from the hustle and bustle, the pressures and the stress of the modern world. You might even think, "These people wouldn't want electricity." You would be wrong.

> *"Living here is very hard. There is no living without electricity", Hamma tells me. "With electricity you can prepare food easier, make juices and even coffee. You have tools to make a window, you can lighten your house and you can have a water pump, you can build a shower and a restroom. And if you do not have electricity, how? You can't do it with a candle."*

The problem is that the family still has the same needs that we do just fewer means of meeting them. They still need to cook their meals and have to perform all the farming and manufacturing activity, but they have to rely on manual or animal labor. They still need water for themselves, for the animals and for irrigation, but they have to get it without electric pumps.

The family still has to have light at night, so Rkia does her homework by candlelight. They own two small gas-fired lamps. One is in the main room where the family sleeps. The other is in the cooking area and casts a light on one of the gravest problems of living without modern sources of energy – indoor cooking over an open fire.

Almost half of the world's population cooks food on open fires indoors. Usually they burn coal, wood or animal dung because they don't have electricity or gas. This results in respiratory illness, and is a major global health problem. The World Health Organization (WHO) estimates that in Africa, indoor smoke from solid fuels is responsible for pulmonary and respiratory problems that result in around half a million early deaths every year. And the sad truth is that half of those who die are poor children exposed to indoor air pollution. They spend most of their time at home breathing in smoke and soot from open fires or leaky coal or wood cook stoves.

Girl in Issidan Izdar by the wood cooking fire

For someone living in a rich country, indoor air pollution is not what you think of when you mention environmental problems. That is expected, since indoor air pollution is not a major concern for most dwellings in America. But if you think about environmental problems as an issue about making the world more livable and safe for humans, then it is obvious that indoor smoke is an environmental problem - in many ways a much bigger problem than the problems of industrial pollution.

Worldwide, 4.3 million people die prematurely from illness attributed to indoor air pollution caused by solid fuels, according to the WHO. Over half of deaths among children younger than five years old are due to pneumonia by soot inhaled indoors.

At the University of Southampton, I met AbuBakr Bahaj, a soft-spoken but passionate Professor of Sustainable Energy, who is one of the world's leading experts on electricity in the developing world. I asked him to describe it for me. *"It's a matter of life and death in many countries,"* he pointed out.

> *"The impact of not having energy relates to transportation and to communication. It's related to water purification and to waste and energy containment. It also relates to agriculture. If you have energy you can pump water for drip irrigation and so forth. Living without electricity makes everything more difficult. You don't have any powered water wells and of course you can't refrigerate the food. Any kind of farming or manufacturing activity must be done with animal or manual labor. And if you don't have electricity to light up your home then you're basically in the dark after 6 o'clock or use something which is much more polluting like kerosene for lighting."*

Bahaj also points out that health care cannot function without electricity.

> *"To run a health clinic you need to be able to sterilize the equipment. You need to have lighting, for example for delivery of a child in the middle of the night. One of the major issues is medication and the storage of medicine. It's actually very difficult to do without refrigerators when a medicine has to be kept at four degrees centigrade. And if you don't have the infrastructure you can't get the vaccine to where it needs to be."*

11

Abu Bakr Bahaj, Professor of Sustainable Energy,
Southampton University, U.K.

The difference modern energy sources make to wellbeing can be traced in the data. Electrified Bangladeshi villages have a 35 percent lower child mortality rate than non-electrified ones, even though the children have similar diseases. Apart from the factors Bahaj mentions above, researchers often talk about how the introduction of radio and television provides inhabitants of electrified villages with better information about healthcare, health, and hygiene. The Bangladeshi study indicates that the lives of 100 children in Bangladesh would be saved each day if the non-electrified villages gained access to modern forms of energy production.A World Bank simulation based on differences between parts of India on and off the grid shows that when electricity is introduced the lives of 7.7 children per thousand born are saved. This means that almost 8,000 children die per million born because of a lack of electricity. This also clearly underestimates the benefits, since electrification also improves the economy and technology long-term, which also has tremendous health benefits. [iv]

Shikha Dalmia, Columnist and Senior Analyst, Reason Foundation

Shikha Dalmia, a columnist and policy analyst at the Reason Foundation in Washington, D.C., born and raised in India, tells me about how people there get by without access to electricity:

> *"Literally it's a question of life and death for poor people in India. You can't easily boil water to get rid of the contamination so a lot of water borne diseases are passed around in rural areas.*
>
> *Mothers will cut down trees for boiling water and preparing food so they rely on the most primitive and most environmentally damaging forms of energy. This also diminishes their quality of life because so much of their time, their daily routine, is occupied by providing this energy that it leaves them very little time to do anything else that's productive.*
>
> *One result is that these countries remain poorer and, when they remain poorer, they then have less money to invest in other environmentally conscious projects."*

When I recently visited New Delhi, one of the cities in India with the best access to electricity, I asked a few locals about how they experienced the world's biggest power outage. I was thinking of the enormous blackout on July 31, 2012, which took 32 gigawatts of generating capacity offline. Incredibly, 620 million people were affected.

The most common response to my question was "What blackout?" Because those who have access to electricity are used to constant blackouts, and they didn't even notice that one was so large that it got international attention. This is inconvenient for households and a disaster for business. Dalmia explains:

> *"If companies and factories can't rely on uninterrupted power around the clock it imposes a huge drag on their productivity. Factories have to shut down production. In the IT industry computers shut down and you lose a lot of your work. In India, businesses that can afford to have started installing their own power generators and backups. But, they come at a cost and produce an economic loss for these companies."*

AbuBakr Bahaj, the Professor of Sustainable Energy in Southampton, grew up without access to electricity in a village called Habban in Yemen. All the work on the farms and in the homes had to be done without the help of powered tools and appliances. As a child he and his brothers had to walk a great distance to a very deep well and pull drinking water up by hand.

When he was 12, the village was electrified. They got electric lights and electric pumps so that they could just turn on the tap to get the water they needed. Refrigeration made it possible to store meat and produce. This created new business opportunities. New goods and services appeared, the villagers ground the grain and tailored the clothes, and they exchanged the results. *"You could see the invigoration of the village around us."*

That change is now taking place in Morocco as well. Electricity is now reaching even the remotest villages in Morocco. The country's National Office of Electricity has a plan to bring power to all villages within the next couple of years. When I travel around the country I see new power lines being drawn, in the desert, and over the roads, sometimes by the power company, sometimes informally by villagers.

A few kilometers away from Issidan Izdar, Hamma's village, is the larger village of Tamayousst. Here things are changing. Tamayousst was wired to the national power grid eight years ago. It has made a huge and positive change in the lives of the villagers.

When I enter a house in Tamayousst I immediately find it far more convenient than Hamma's in Issidan Izdar. There is a light in the bathroom and a shower, something you don't appreciate until it's not there. The food in this house is fresh and uncontaminated because there is a refrigerator. Most importantly, there is a modern kitchen with running water for cooking and cleaning up. And because the family cooks meals on a gas stove, this family is not burning wood indoors and exposing themselves to dangerous smoke.

According to Abderrahmane Ait Braim, the village Imam in Tamayousst, electricity has not just improved the economy, it has "brought a lot of happiness:"

> *"When we got electricity it was like a big party in the village. People were happy with lights in the house, they were happy to watch television. They were happy with streetlights, to have refrigerators and appliances. Electricity brought everyone in the village much happiness."*

In Tamayousst there are electric lights so that families can read or socialize after dark. They can watch television and see news from Morocco and the rest of the world. People have cell phones and can communicate with those outside of the village. Some own computers and can access programs they want to watch, in their own language.

Village Imam and two other men watching comedy on laptop

This little tale of two villages in Morocco gave me a very visual and also emotional insight into the importance of electricity to lift people out of poverty. Lacking electricity makes every daily routine much more difficult. Reliable access to electricity in India would transform life in India tremendously, Shikha Dalmia points out:

> *"Factories would be able to run uninterrupted so their productivity would go up. Mothers would be able to boil the water and prepare their foods in a hygienic way that would cut down the rate of disease. It would completely transform the way people actually arrange their lives around the supply of energy today."*

Paradoxically, it is this very hope that worries many in the western world. As more people get richer and gain access to electricity and modern goods and services, they also create new environmental problems.

When electricity is produced directly from fossil fuels - or coal, petroleum or natural gas - the result is a growth in carbon dioxide (CO_2) emissions. From 2005 through 2011, China added about two 600-megawatt coal plants a week. U. S. government projects that China will build a new major coal power plant every 10 days for the next 10 years, the most carbon-intense energy source. China burns more than 4 billion tons of coal. The U.S. burns less than 1 billion, and the European Union burns 600 million.

China's increased coal consumption is happening at light speed. In 2006 China passed America as the biggest emitter of carbon dioxide from energy production. Just eight years later China already emitted almost twice what America did.

But we must remember that this is also the development that has resulted in an unprecedented poverty reduction in China and elsewhere. The most recent World Bank data show that more than 115 million people were raised out of extreme poverty. In other words, 220 people were liberated from poverty every minute of every day. And this is a long-term trend.

In the last 30 years extreme poverty has been reduced from 53 to 17 percent of the developing world population. Even though world population has grown by around 2.5 billion people, there are now almost one billion fewer who live in extreme poverty. This means more infants are saved, more children can go to school instead of work and more parents can feed themselves and their families. As they create new environmental threats from manufacturing and transport, they also solve the ancient environmental threats that kill millions every year – indoor air pollution, dirty water, lack of sanitation facilities.

AbuBakr Bahaj, the Professor of Sustainable Energy, puts it this way:

> *"There are people who feel that expansion of technology into remote areas will maybe have more impact on the environment and that we shouldn't do it. I think these people are perhaps not thinking very seriously about the wellbeing of*

those communities. Those communities have aspirations like anybody else; they want to develop and they want to make progress."

Climate change

Following the public discourse on climate change as a layman, it often appears as a very black and white dispute. Either you believe in it or you don't. If you do, it's a matter of life and death for humanity. If you don't, you don't acknowledge any problems whatsoever with a rise in greenhouse gases or a warming climate.

If you don't have a dog in this fight, it's easy to see that the issue is more complex. First of all, few people seriously involved in studying climate change are questioning the basic premise that emissions of carbon dioxide and other so called greenhouse gases affect the global climate. That effect will make the world warmer than otherwise would be the case.

So our present understanding of the science involved is clear and simple: more carbon dioxide in the atmosphere will make for a warmer climate. But the science is not clear or simple when you ask the next question: to what degree and in which time frame will more carbon dioxide make it warmer?

It makes a huge difference if global temperatures will rise one degree Celsius or five degrees in the next hundred years. There is a broad spectrum of possible outcomes, from minor and even beneficial changes to global disaster. Increased carbon dioxide in the air has a positive effect on plants and increases global biomass production' Despite what we hear during every heat wave, more people die because of cold weather than warm.

If the temperature increases too much it might lead to floods, droughts, eradication of species, tropical diseases, hurricanes, and rapidly melting glaciers – all becoming more frequent. The consequences and the costs may be very large, especially in the poor countries of the world - which do not have the resources and technology necessary to handle rapid adjustments.

In less likelier worst-case scenarios, there are feedback loops that lead to the fear that climate is spinning out of control. Higher temperatures would, for example, melt the northern permafrost tundra releasing vast amounts of the greenhouse gas methane and melting ice sheets that provide earth with solar reflectivity, thus accelerating the change.

At this time it's fair to say that science can make more or less educated guesses based on advanced computer models. The good news is that the various predictions of these models so far have proven to be on the high side. The empirical evidence – the actual temperatures measured – is less dramatic than the forecasts of the models. For more than one-and one- half decades global temperatures have, on average, been the same.

The next step in evaluating the importance of climate change is, however, even more complex than the rather straightforward science involved. If we accept, as I believe we should, that human-induced climate change is a reality, what would be an appropriate and realistic strategy for managing it? If adapting to higher temperatures and other possible negative consequences of releasing carbon dioxide to the atmosphere is less costly than reducing emissions, then adapting is not only an acceptable but also a sensible choice of action.

It is, of course, rational to limit emissions of carbon dioxide *ceteris paribus*, as economists say (everything else being equal). It might be sensible to put a price on emissions – I will return to that issue later in the book. Even if a worst-case scenario might be very unlikely, it is worth something to insure ourselves against it by limiting global warming. You don't have to believe that the house will burn down to buy insurance against it.

However, far-reaching domestic regulatory efforts to limit carbon dioxide emissions might be counterproductive. It is not necessarily true that the best way forward is to limit emissions of greenhouse gases to such an extent as to prevent climate change. If climate change is judged not to be catastrophic in the short- or medium-term time frame then adapting to it could and should be on the public agenda.

Resources that would be consumed to reduce emissions must be weighed against what it would cost to adapt to climate change or to invest in basic energy research or new energy technologies that have the potential to end our present dependence on fossil fuels.

What is important is that our climate policies don't hurt our ability to create more wealth, better technologies and to bring power to the world's poor. That would be a case of ridding the patient of the disease by killing him. The biggest problems in the world are still problems of poverty and traditional environmental problems, like bad indoor air and polluted water. Forcing too many restraints and costs on today's global population might be a way of hurting people and making life more difficult for the poor today because we want to reduce the risks to tomorrow's rich.

If annual global economic growth remains around 2 percent per head, in one hundred years' time the average person will be around eight times richer than today's average person. This is particularly important since there is a risk that the worst damage will occur in poor countries, in part as a direct result of their poverty. With those resources, the level of scientific knowledge, and the technological solutions that may then be at our disposal, many of the problems that intimidate us today will be much easier to handle – from adapting to warming to taking CO_2 out of the atmosphere.

Continuous economic development will also give us better tools to deal with all kinds of threats to life and nature, whether they be man-made global warming or recurrent pandemics, earthquakes, tsunamis, super-volcanic eruptions, meteorite impacts or natural climate changes. Banking everything on countering one single risk will make us more vulnerable to other problems, even if that particular risk, according to present-day computer models, is the worst one of all.

It will be costly to get power to the 1.3 billion people around the world that lack electricity, and one of those costs is environmental. But we have to ask ourselves, doesn't the world's poor deserve the same kind of life-changing benefits that power has brought the developed world? And in the end, it doesn't really matter what we think. People in developing nations are going to seek lives with our levels of abundant energy. It is happening now.

The future of energy and of global environmental problems will not depend that much on what we do in industrialized countries belonging to the Organization for Economic Co-operation and

Development (OECD). According to the International Energy Agency global energy demand will increase by over 50 percent until 2035 on current trends. The proportion of CO_2 emissions that come from the rich countries is already below 50 percent, down from almost 100 percent in the beginning of the 20th century. They have basically stopped growing, and as currently trending, will be down to less than a quarter by the end of the century.

North America, Europe, Australia and Japan could abandon all fossil fuels, dismantle all their industries and halt all forms of transportation, and the world would still increase CO_2 emissions during the next 40 years.

No end in sight

Not even in the rich world do we see any serious reduction in energy use. It's tempting to think that we are approaching an era in the developed world of a less materialistic economy. In this new age, we will produce fewer things and more ideas. For example we might spend more of our time communicating and being online rather than travelling in real life. It is true that the use of energy per capita seems to rise less quickly as we get richer.

The amount of energy required to produce a unit of wealth in the western world has declined by around one percent per year in the past 150 years, and that pace has accelerated. If technology in the United States had been frozen at the 1900 level, Americans would be emitting three times more CO_2 than they actually do today.

Although we have made great strides in making everything more energy efficient - from jumbo jets to television sets - we've increased our use of energy. Not only are there more people who fly more, but there's a TV set - even an Internet terminal - on the back of the seat in the airplane.

Internet requires that we build computers, network connections and cell-phone towers. The internet runs on data centers, air conditioned to keep machines operating at safe temperatures. It's been estimated that the internet uses somewhere between four and six percent of the world's total electrical output, and it is increasing rapidly.

In North America and Europe many are exploring lifestyle choices that are more local and small-scale, for environmental reasons, but a closer look reveals that it is not always greener. Buying food grown in rural areas outside of your hometown will help the local farmer and put healthy, fresh vegetables and fruits on your table. But if both you and the farmer drive to and from the market, you might end up using more energy than you think - possibly more than if you bought your food at the supermarket, where it's transported from much farther away, but in bulk, thereby using less energy.

Some think that we're just using too much energy. Maybe we could move to a simpler time and demand less from the power grid. If we all just lived with less, closer to nature, that would have a major effect on our need for energy, and a positive impact on the environment. Right?

The Three Rivers Recreation Area - in central Oregon - is a large natural environment with 700 homes on thousands of remote acres. Everybody in this breathtakingly beautiful river landscape live "off the grid." They've chosen to build here even though there are no utility services: no electrical power, no water and no sewer.

However, it's not at all what you expect. The residents live comfortable lives, with access to most of the technologies we take for granted, but powered by solar panels and batteries. They have refrigerators and washing machines, cars and motorboats. When I visited the people who live there it was difficult to see that their houses are off the grid. It's tempting to think that more of us could live like this. Elaine Budden, who moved there with her husband in 1995, tells me *"I don't want to oversimplify it, but it's a piece of cake."*

Everyone I talked to thought that moving there was a wonderful choice. *"It's a little, little bit of heaven,"* says one.

Although I appreciate the lifestyle in Three Rivers - independent and close to an amazing nature - I don't think this is the way forward for us all. One reason is that it's costly. A solar system for a small home can cost $15,000, and for a high-end home even $40,000 - that is a huge upfront investment. Another is that the lifestyle seems to work better in a rural setting, with little density.

"I don't think this would ever work in downtown Portland," Ralph

Johnson says. He and his wife bought their first property in Three Rivers in 1975, and moved there permanently from Portland in 1999.

"First of all: I don't know if they would allow you to start storing up big banks of batteries and then solar panels all over the yards. And then having a diesel generator coming on in the middle of the night with your neighbor 50 feet away? That'd drive your neighbor crazy. I just don't see it in a metropolitan area. It's going to have to be pretty rural."

Another consideration is that it isn't certain they are actually saving energy. Yes, they are powered by the sun, but also by diesel generators when the sun doesn't shine. Water heaters, stoves and furnaces are powered by propane, which emits almost as much carbon dioxide as gasoline. And they have to drive far to buy food – and even to get to the mailbox.

Energy conservation is a good thing and may be a necessary part of our energy future. There is no sense in using energy that you don't need. So turn the lights off and don't heat an empty house. Perhaps new network technologies can help us do this automatically. But it takes an industrialized society to make solar panels, battery banks, generators and propane. Even living off the grid, requires a grid.

Many of our perceptions about energy use are wrong. Which part of the United States is the greenest? Most people think of something rural and small-scale but, in fact, New York is a very green city. Surprisingly, Manhattan has the lowest carbon footprint in the country. Individually, New Yorkers use less than half of the electricity that the average American does, and as little gasoline as the rest of the country did in the 1920's.

Why is New York City so green? Because population density reduces energy, water use and the generation of solid waste. Apartment buildings might not look very green, but they are the most energy efficient form of housing. When you heat them, you are not just warming wildlife, but also your neighbors. More than half of New Yorkers commute by mass transit and you don't have to drive much because you can buy literally anything, right around the corner.

But even in New York, the usage of energy is increasing while we get richer, live longer and do more things with our lives. And, the rest

23

of the world wants our chances as well. Whatever we do next - whether we create full-immersion virtual reality or cure cancer, extend life spans even further, or go into space - it will take more energy, not less.

We can't go back. There is too much at stake for too many people. And the most is at stake in the poorest countries. Hamma and his family in Issidan Izdar deserve the same kind of life we lead. And, whatever we think about it, they are working hard to get it. The only thing we might be able to affect is how they do it, and which technologies they use.

i. E. A. Wrigley, Energy and the English Industrial Revolution (Cambridge: Cambridge University Press, 2010). David S. Landes, The Unbound Prometheus : Technological Change and Industrial Development in Western Europe from 1750 to the Present. Cambridge University Press. Second edition, 2003, p. 98.

ii. Matt Ridley, The Rational Optimist: How Prosperity Evolves, London: Fourth Estate, 2010, p. 236.

iii. http://www.youtube.com/watch?v=6sqnptxlCcw

iv. Bas van der Klaauw & Limin Wang, "Child Mortality in Rural India", World bank, 2009.

~ ~ ~

2. What are our energy options?

"We will chase perfection, and we will chase it relentlessly, knowing all the while we can never attain it. But along the way, we shall catch excellence."

Vince Lombardi

More people than ever, with higher living standards than ever, will need more energy, much more. From where?

In a way, energy is not scarce, it's everywhere. The world is turning, the wind is blowing and water is flowing downhill. The sun is powered by nuclear reactions and just one hour of sunlight equals all of mankind's electricity usage for a year if we could capture it all.

Plants use the sun's energy to grow. Some animals power themselves by eating those plants and others by eating those herbivores. Over millions of years, heat and pressure turned buried plants and animals into fossil fuels, like coal and oil.

The world is overflowing with energy. The bottleneck is our ability to safely convert, store and pay for it. Researchers and entrepreneurs are constantly hard at work to improve every aspect of all of these sources, to get more energy from them at a cheaper price and with less damage to people and nature.

Many have their own favorite energy sources, for economic or ideological reasons, and say that there is only one way to go. But for an outside, disinterested observer, it seems like every energy source that we have discovered has its limitations and its environmental impacts. There are benefits and there are problems with them all. Let's take a look.

Coal

Coal is the mother of power to the people. Although humans have used coal, like they have used wood charcoal, for thousands of years, the big leap in the use of coal came with the industrial revolution in the mid-18th century. At that time. around 80 percent of the world's coal was mined in Britain.

Coal is fossilized plant or algae matter that has been buried deep in the earth for millions of years. The pressure and the intense heat at those depths have turned vegetation into a hard black material that primarily consists of carbon.

As the industrial revolution took hold in more and more countries and the use of coal exploded, worries started to grow about the fact that coal, after all, is a finite, non-renewable resource. As early as the second half of the 19th century many wondered whether coal use was sustainable and asked when stocks of coal would be exhausted. One of the leading economists of the era, Stanley Jevons, wrote the book *The Coal Question* in 1865, in which he warned about peaking coal usage – Britain would suffer tremendously because it would run out of its primary energy resource.

Still, 150 years later some would say that the problem with coal is not that it's finite, but that there is a lot of it. So much in fact that the use of coal is still growing. During the last decade, almost half of the world's additional energy demand was provided by coal.

It is estimated that proven coal reserves worldwide (what is considered economically recoverable at any given time, taking into account available mining technology and costs) are over 180 billion tons. That is enough coal to last for more than 100 years at current rates of production. It should be added that calculations of total coal resources (all potential coal deposits) add up to over 17,000 billion tons. That is equivalent to another 2,000 years of production.

Therefore, the biggest benefit of coal is that we will not run out of it in the foreseeable future. Coal stands for 30 percent of global primary energy consumption and 40 percent of the world's electricity generation - that is a key aspect. In the US about half of the electricity generation is coal based.

Most of the increase in coal consumption takes place in rapidly emerging countries. China alone now burns almost as much coal as the rest of the world combined. Whereas US coal production has leveled off around one billion tons a year, China has doubled its yearly production to over 3500 tons in only ten years. And, it is on course to double its number of coal-fired plants by 2040. Before the market reforms of the late 1970's in China, production was less than 500,000 tons.

Another giant following China is India. Although India is having problems expanding its coal mining industry to keep up with demand, it's already the world's third largest coal consumer. With India's present plans for expanding coal-generated electricity, the country is set to more than double its coal consumption over the next two decades.

It's obvious that coal is going to have to continue to be part of the energy mix for some time because it's so dominant, so abundant and so cheap. So what is the problem?

Coal is dirty. Both the production and use of coal is closely related to major negative environmental impacts. The use of so-called strip or surface mining is highly controversial in developed countries. It scars the landscape, damages water resources and it's costly to fix abandoned mines. In developing countries coal mining is also a dangerous trade with over 1,000 miners dying in accidents per year, just in China.

Coal Plant near Berlin

The biggest problem of coal is burning it. The emissions include sulfur dioxide, nitrogen oxides, particulates and many toxic elements

27

like mercury. And then, of course, large quantities of the most important greenhouse gas - carbon dioxide.

Someone old enough to have lived in London when coal was burned in every stove in every house, will vividly remember the famous London smog. The very specific smell produced by burning coal - especially coal of poor quality - was part of living in the countries of the former Soviet empire before the fall of the Berlin Wall. Now, the smog and smell of coal is a sign of development in many parts of the world. And although coal is better than burning wood and dung, the negative effects on human health are still immense. In China many hundreds of thousand die prematurely from air pollution every year, air pollution mainly emanating from coal use. In many Chinese cities the smog often gets so bad that breathing the air constitutes an acute health danger.

With increased resources and new technologies coal can become less dirty, if not clean. In China the use of coal in smaller settings, such as private homes. It is being banned in many locations and being replaced by electricity generated by new coal-fired power plants that use advanced methods to limit pollution. For example, adding up-to-date filtering would go a long way to make breathing easier in China's rapidly growing cities. Carbon capture and sequestration could possibly be used on a larger scale, even though it is expensive with today's technology.

Oil

If coal is the mother of power to the people, then oil – or petroleum – is the next generation. Today oil is the most important part of the global energy supply as it makes up almost a third. However, it is likely that coal, because of its increased use in rapidly developing economies, will overtake oil in the near future and once again become the most important source of energy.

Although oil in many ways is just liquid coal, fundamentally created the same way eons ago by large quantities of dead organisms, its main use is different. To some small extent oil is also used for heating and generating electricity, but its chief importance is to power transportation in its different refined forms as gasoline, diesel and jet fuel. Historically the use of oil is therefore closely connected to the invention of the internal combustion engine in the late 19th century and the following rise of the automotive industry. After the Second World War the development of commercial aviation contributed to the use of oil. But, even today, aviation (including military aircraft) accounts for only about six percent of oil consumption.

For those of us who own a car, the cost of energy – or power – becomes unpleasantly concrete when it comes to oil. Every time you go to a gas station to "fill 'er up" you notice the price per gallon that is more or less directly connected to the constant swings in the world-market price for oil. For us Europeans the price of gas is particularly noticeable since most of the cost is actually not an outcome of the market for oil, but of taxes. A gallon of gas in Sweden – like in most of Europe – is seven to eight dollars, of which more than half is taxes. In the US the average tax per gallon is 50 cents.

The way we are regularly reminded of the price of a gallon of gas also make us conscious of the finite character of oil. Oil is, of course, a non-renewable energy source. Still, the actual amount of oil in the ground has little to do with the day-to-day price of oil.

When the first oil crisis shook the world in 1973, and the price of a barrel of oil (42 gallons or 159 liters) went from three to 12 dollars in less than six months, it had nothing to do with a physical shortage of oil. The price hike was the result of politically motivated actions by a group of the largest oil producing countries, situated in the Middle East. As a response to US involvement in the Yom Kippur War, the Arab countries declared an oil embargo against a number of western countries.

The embargo, amplified with unwise domestic policies such as price controls and rationing, not only led to severe economic consequences, but also to anxiety about the end of oil. The oil crisis was seen as a rehearsal for a forthcoming and inevitable real shortage of oil. In a US context this was particularly understandable, since US oil production had peaked in 1970.

A report, *The Limits to Growth*, published in 1972 by the global think tank Club of Rome, gave these worries an intellectual foundation and considerable media attention. Using computer models based on exponential economic and population growth combined with limited stocks, the report proposed that a number of essential natural resources would be exhausted in just a few decades. In the case of oil the last drops would be consumed in 1992 according to the computer results.

Just like earlier warnings about coal, these fateful predictions about the end of oil have not materialized. Proven oil reserves are actually 70 percent higher today than they were 20 years ago, even though a lot of oil has been consumed during that time. In 1992, proven reserves amounted to 1,000 billion barrels, and in 2012 reserves were 1,700 billion barrels. This is sufficient for another half century of present global production.

The technology for finding and extracting oil is improving constantly. When the price of oil is high it creates an incentive for innovation. For example, drilling ships are being built that can operate in 10,000 feet of water, and then drill down another 40,000 feet into the earth for oil – much more than the height of Mount Everest. Those ships can hold steady and continue drilling even in waves of up to 30 feet. And now, hydraulic fracturing is letting us access oil in shale, which has increased US oil production dramatically.

If we look beyond proven reserves – that is, reserves claimed to have a reasonable certainty (over 90 percent probability) of being recoverable under existing economic and political conditions with existing technology – there are a lot more reserves. So-called unconventional oil, basically any oil not produced by the standard oil well method, should also be considered. There are huge quantities of heavy oil, oil shale and oil sand.

In Canada and Venezuela it is estimated that there are at least 3,500 billion barrels of unconventional oil in the form of oil sands. All of that is not recoverable. But with current technology, official calculations project that about ten percent will be available for extraction, adding several hundred billion barrels in reserves in just these two countries. This places Canada and Venezuela in the same league as Saudi Arabia, having the three largest oil reserves in the world.

One problem with oil is that we have often relied on some of the most authoritarian regimes in the world to satisfy our demand for it, like Iran, Saudi Arabia, Venezuela and Russia. Since those governments control the oil resources, high oil prices make them stronger and more in control of their societies. The New York Times columnist Thomas Friedman has even suggested "The First Law of Petropolitics."

> *"The price of oil and the pace of freedom always move in opposite directions in oil-rich petrolist states. According to the First Law of Petropolitics, the higher the average global crude oil price rises, the more free speech, free press, free and fair elections, an independent judiciary, the rule of law, and independent political parties are eroded. And these negative trends are reinforced by the fact that the higher the price goes, the less petrolist leaders are sensitive to what the world thinks or says about them.*

> *Conversely, according to the First Law of Petropolitics, the lower the price of oil, the more petrolist countries are forced to move toward a political system and a society that is more transparent, more sensitive to opposition voices, and more focused on building the legal and educational structures that will maximize their people's ability, both men's and women's, to compete, start new companies, and attract investments from abroad. The lower the price of crude oil falls, the more petrolist leaders are sensitive to what outside forces think of them."* [v]

To Friedman, this is an argument to move to other renewable energy sources, but it can also be used as an argument for democracies to develop domestic oil resources more effectively.

It could be said of oil, as of coal, that from an environmental point of view, the main problem is that there is so much of it. At every stage of the process, from production to consumption, oil causes negative effects on the environment. As a fossil fuel the main focus is on the large emissions of carbon dioxide. But oil pollutes in many ways and perhaps the most dramatic are the regularly occurring oil spills. One of the worst – the 2010 Deepwater Horizon oil spill in the Gulf of Mexico – produced an environmental disaster with vast consequences. Almost five billion barrels of crude oil were accidently released into the ocean.

At the same time, better technology and security have resulted in a reduction in the number of accidental oil spills from tankers, combined carriers and barges by more than 90 percent since the 1970's. Even though we transport and use more oil than ever, less than four percent of all the oil spilled since 1970 was spilled in the last decade. [vi]

Natural Gas

Natural gas is the third most important source for power. Just like coal and oil, it is a fossil fuel – the remains of dead animals and plants exposed to pressure and heat over millennia. Impurities are removed and then it is used for heating, cooking and electricity generation. More than one-fifth of the global primary energy supply comes from natural gas, and it's growing in importance.

At one time, natural gas was more of a nuisance than a valuable source of energy. Since natural gas often exists in the same wells as oil, it was an unwanted byproduct in oil fields if there was no market for gas close to the production areas. Natural gas had to be piped to consumers, and therefore most of the gas was simply burned off. Today such unwanted gas is usually returned to the reservoir.

As with coal and oil, there is an abundance of natural gas and proven reserves are increasing as we consume more and more gas. In 2012 proven reserves stood at 6,600 trillion cubic feet, sufficient to meet 56 years of global production. Natural gas is comparatively cheap and it's easy to build gas-fired electrical power stations.

Natural gas is virtually clean, and unlike coal and oil, it doesn't produce many pollutants. From a global warming perspective, it has a major benefit. Burning natural gas produce less carbon dioxide, three-quarters of what oil produces and around 45 percent of what coal produces per unit of energy. However, natural gas does contain methane and when that leaks into the atmosphere - which is often the case during extraction - it is an even more powerful greenhouse gas than CO_2. However, methane is also removed from the atmosphere after some ten years due to oxidation, while CO_2 stays for a century or more.

A better method of tracking leaks with infrared cameras, and even satellites, in addition to improved systems for capturing the gas would help would help make natural gas use more effective. It could even be profitable. BP has introduced methane-catching systems at 2,300 well sites in New Mexico. Gas that used to escape now flows through meters that the crews call "the cash register." Reid Smith from BP points out:

> *"We spend a lot of money to get gas to the surface. It makes a huge amount of sense to get all of it through the sales meter."*
> [vii]

In the US natural gas has become a game changer in the energy sector. Natural gas trapped within shale formations – shale gas – has become increasingly recoverable thanks to new technology like hydraulic fracturing and horizontal drilling. In 2000 shale gas provided one percent of US natural gas production. Now the shale gas share is around 40 percent of natural gas production.

Actually the US and Canada are the only major global producers of commercially viable natural gas from shale formations, but the extraction of shale gas is possible in other parts of the world and expected to grow rapidly in the coming years.

In Europe, natural gas is also an important part of the energy mixture, but Europe is heavily dependent on importing from Russia. This is increasingly seen as a problem as the relationship between Russia and Europe has deteriorated. Therefore, a number of European countries look to shale gas as an alternative. They would also welcome US competition in the form of liquefied natural gas exports, which have so far been stifled by regulation. A number of large gas liquefaction projects are on their way in the US and exports are expected to start soon. Some even predict that US gas exports could ultimately exceed Russian exports to Europe.

Natural-gas-powered plants now generate 30 percent of US electricity, a doubling since the beginning of the century. This rapid expansion has made it possible to bring down the use of coal, which has led to substantially lower US emissions of greenhouse gases.

Still, natural gas does produce CO_2 emissions, and as its use is increasing it is becoming a bigger contributor to greenhouse gases in the atmosphere. Environmental concerns connected to the shale gas boom are also growing since hydraulic fracturing requires large quantities of water as well as the use of chemicals.

Biomass

In many European countries, subsidies for renewables have resulted in a revival of what could be called mankind's original energy source: burning wood or, rather, using biomass. In my hometown of Malmö in Sweden, the "district heat" authority uses wood and waste - like trash - to deliver much of the city's heat requirements. In Germany, almost 40 percent of the renewable energy demand comes from biomass - from sticks to pellet. Old power stations can be adapted to burn wood, which doesn't require any backup power.

In most of the world biomass is chiefly used in the old way. Currently biomass covers approximately one-tenth of the global energy supply. Two-thirds of that is used in developing countries for cooking and heating. (One should note that all the statistics about global energy supply and use are based on more or less reliable data. The use of wood, for example, is even more difficult to measure, since it is often part of an informal economy.)

So you could say that there is old and new biomass use. Old biomass use is often ineffective, threatens the environment and causes major health problems. New biomass, however, holds a lot of promise. New technologies make it possible to produce power from biomass in more efficient and cleaner ways than before. In principle, if we grow as much biomass as we use, it should be carbon dioxide neutral in theory.

The problem is that biomass being carbon neutral is not always the case. Wood needs energy when it is processed, when it is shipped and in the power station. Whether it is carbon neutral depends on the type of trees used and how fast they grow. One study showed that using whole trees for energy increases carbon emissions (compared with coal) by 79 percent over 20 years, and 49 percent over 40 years. There is no carbon reduction at all until around 100 years, when the new trees have matured. So the irony is that we actually increase CO_2 emissions in the foreseeable future. "Environmental lunacy in Europe", as *The Economist* describes it. [viii]

Wood chip plant, Sweden

Bio-energy is also more expensive than other alternatives and the large-scale use of biomass often demands that huge areas of land be set aside. This could damage biological diversity and compete with food production. The land it takes up would probably otherwise have been used for other forms of plants that would have reduced carbon emissions. We already see a strain on trees in Europe. Furniture-makers complain that they are being destroyed by surging prices, and Europe is importing much more wood from other parts of the world.

But research is ongoing. Perhaps we can genetically modify trees so they grow faster. In the future it might be possible that biomass will play a major role in production of fuels for transportation. We might create bio-energy through processes using algae or bacteria. Since 2011 biofuels have been approved for commercial aviation use, and some carriers are using it on an experimental basis.

It is even possible that the end of the oil age will come one day when we have some renewable replacement for oil based on biomass. We just haven't figured out the engineering to do it at scale yet and at a reasonable cost.

Nuclear

Nuclear power is the energy that is derived from the *nucleus*, the core, of the atom. In a nuclear fission reactor, atoms are split to release that energy. Around 14 percent of the world's electricity comes from nuclear power, equal to five percent of the total global primary energy supply. Globally there are more than 400 reactors generating electricity. Around 100 nuclear power reactors in the US produce 20 percent of the electricity.

In my own country, Sweden, nuclear plays an even larger role. Ten reactors provide 40 percent of our electricity. In France 58 reactors generate more than 70 percent of the country's electricity. France is the world's largest net exporter of electricity due to its nuclear program.

Nuclear power is presently one of few, if not the only, large-scale alternatives to fossil fuels. It's also one of the least environmentally damaging forms of producing power. Nuclear is clean energy. From a greenhouse perspective it's great, and one of the reasons Sweden has managed to keep carbon dioxide emissions per capita quite low compared to most other developed economies.

Nuclear reactors are of minimal environmental concern when they operate as they should. Unfortunately they do not always do that. If something goes wrong, the consequences can be huge and catastrophic. Incidents like Three Mile Island, Chernobyl and Fukushima have shown us that the impact on society from nuclear accidents can be dramatic and destructive.

The futurologist and technologist Ramez Naam, who is the author of the book *The Infinite Resource* about our energy future, tells me that many concerns are overblown:

> *"Look at Fukushima: we had a tidal wave that killed 10,000 people and we had a nuclear accident that so far killed zero and the World Health Organization says will kill maybe 10 people over the next 40 years. And yet the nuclear accident gets 100 times more coverage on the news as the tsunami that created it. People are irrationally frightened of nuclear. It makes excellent, excellent television and I'm not sure how to fix that unfortunately."*

However, the fear is real and has to be taken into account. Another issue that has followed nuclear power as a dark shadow since the beginning is the possible connection between the civil and military use of nuclear technology, as we have recently seen in the international conflicts surrounding the Iranian nuclear program.

All this has made nuclear power politically controversial. But possibly the main and real reason nuclear is not viewed as the solution to our dependence on fossil fuels is that it is not sufficiently competitive. Finding a way to safely store the radioactive waste for thousands and thousands of years has proven difficult.

To a large degree the cost of nuclear power is linked to the building of the reactors and taking care of the spent fuel. Running the reactors is comparatively cheap. Most of the already built reactors are consequently quite profitable, but they are complex, time-consuming and politically sensitive to build. Therefore, to make a business case for developing and building new reactors has become incredibly difficult. It is hard to see it as a short-term response to global warming concerns.

In 2005 a Finnish company decided to construct a new nuclear reactor, making Finland the first Western European country in 15 years to order one. It was estimated that the power plant, Olkiluoto 3, would be up and running in 2010. The latest estimate is that the reactor will be operational in 2018 with total costs for the plant almost three times the original delivery price of four billion dollars.

Hydro

Hydropower is the method of harnessing the energy from falling or running water. Today we do not think of quaint old watermills when talking of hydropower, but of large dams and power stations. Of the world's primary energy supply, hydropower represents 2.4 percent. About ten percent of the electricity in the US is generated by hydropower.

Hydropower has expanded rapidly. Over the last 50 years the world has constructed two large dams per day, half of those in China. It's clean power. It doesn't produce greenhouse gases or add pollutants to rivers and streams. It's fairly cheap and since we can turn the turbines on and off in minutes it's online whenever we need it.

Building large dams can, however, have substantial environmental side effects. Apart from aesthetic considerations, damming rivers and streams affects aquatic ecosystems. Thanks to our great rivers in the north, hydropower supplies Swedes with almost half of our electricity. But one of the side effects is that we ruined our stocks of salmon. As a result, it has become more common for dam operators to build fish passage and ladder devices to help migrating species.

Bonneville Dam on the Columbia River

Large hydropower projects in developing countries frequently get criticized for destroying pristine nature and undermining the living conditions for inhabitants along the waterways to be flooded. In many instances, it has involved the forceful removal of people who lived there.

One of the most controversial projects, China's Three Gorges Dam, avoids the emissions of something like 100 million tons of carbon dioxide every year. But at the same time, it submerged 13 cities and displaced an incredible 1.3 million people.

In developed nations, the biggest drawback is that the potential to expand hydropower is limited. Practically all the suitable sites for large hydroelectric dams are already in use. It is difficult to see how large-scale hydroelectric power can be increased further.

Wind

The step from traditional windmills to contemporary wind turbines might be short in principle, but in practice modern wind power is altogether different.

It's difficult to think of a cleaner way of generating power than harnessing the wind. But currently wind supplies no more than one percent of energy globally and less than four percent of the electricity.

Some countries have gone further. Denmark was a forerunner in developing wind power. Wind turbines today supply the country with almost a third of its electricity needs. The plan is to increase that share to 50 percent by 2020.

Wind power is a capital-intensive power source. The wind is free, but the wind turbines are not. Wind farms are often small-scale and located far from the consumers, so it presupposes investments in new transmission lines. Offshore generators are even more expensive, since they operate in a corrosive environment, are difficult to maintain and repair, and require underwater cables.

In 1984 Christopher Flavin at the Worldwatch Institute said that *"Tax credits have been essential to the economic viability of wind farms so far, but will not be needed within a few years"*. The technology is still heavily subsidized.

The biggest drawback with wind power is that the wind is intermittent. It doesn't blow all the time and for turbines to work at full capacity the wind must be strong. However it can't be too strong either. Generators are actually designed to feather their props when the wind gets too strong.

Wind power consequently has to be backed up with some other power source that can be speedily turned off and on, like hydropower or turbines running on natural gas. This can add significantly to the costs.

We would have to build 140 very large wind turbines every day, just to match the annual *increase* in China's carbon dioxide emissions from coal. If we were to compensate for all their fossil fuels - Latin America's and our own - we would quickly run out of money to build wind turbines as well as the land and shallow sea beds on which they're built. This sets another limit to its expansion.

As wind power technology expands, popular resistance continues to mount against the environmental impact on the beauty of the landscape. Additionally, it has been estimated that almost half a million birds are killed annually by wind power in the US alone.

Solar

Every hour of every day the sun beams more than enough energy onto the Earth to satisfy global energy needs for an entire year. Considering this, together with the fact that the sun is not about to go out in the foreseeable future, we really should not need to worry about power to the people.

It's only a question of turning the light from the sun into forms of energy that we can easily use. This has become possible with the invention of photovoltaic cells, or solar cells, which directly convert sunlight into electricity.

The cost of solar cells has, however, been prohibitive in large-scale applications compared to the alternatives. But just as computer chips and computer capacity based on the same technology – semiconducting materials – have become significantly cheaper, solar cells have become more efficient and less expensive. The cost to install solar photovoltaic systems has dropped 40 percent in the last three years.

In certain locations with enough sunlight solar cells make sense from both a practical and economic point of view. In poor countries, far from the grid, solar power can also be a way of creating a small-scale, decentralized system for generating electricity.

Thirty years ago, solar cells could only convert a small percentage of sunlight to electricity. Today's commercial solar cells can convert about 15 percent of the energy in the sunlight into electricity. In the laboratory solar cells have reached energy conversion rates above 40 percent.

Solar energy has many advantages. It's abundant and clean. You can produce it small scale – from a few watts to recharge a cell phone – to large scale – hundreds of megawatts for industrial generation. You can produce it in remote locations. And you can produce it in developing countries when there is a lack of infrastructure.

But solar energy does have negatives. Even though costs are dropping it's still very expensive compared to the alternatives. It doesn't work when the sun doesn't shine and it lacks good storage solutions, and as with wind, it needs a backup system. The production of solar cells is also energy intensive and dependent on the mining of raw materials that are hazardous and can cause health problems.

Apart from solar cells, there are other methods to generate electricity from the sun. One way is by using mirrors to heat a liquid that creates steam to drive a turbine and generate electricity. I have visited such a power plant in the desert of northern Africa - in Morocco - that has the advantage of strong bright sunlight. At that facility they showed me an innovative way of dealing with the storage problem. During the day, the liquid heated by the mirrors also heats salt until it's a molten liquid. The stored heat in the salt then powers the generators for five hours after the sun sets. This will help Morocco get through its evening peak power demand.

It is estimated that the sun shining over the deserts of North Africa contain enough energy to supply 40 times the present world electricity demand.

Solar Panels at Noor 1 Solar Plant, Ouarzazate, Morocco

Trade-offs

So it's clear, every form of energy comes with its own set of problems. Still, we need a lot of it now and we're going to need even more in the years ahead. This should caution all those who are cheerleaders for one solution, above all else. For example, for some reason, the political Left often loves wind power and the Right cheers on nuclear power. To an outsider they look fairly similar - both in the potential of reducing CO_2 and the hurdles of very high costs.

This means we can't rule out any one of the energy sources just because it isn't perfect. The world itself is not perfect, especially not in poor countries, where a lack of energy equals poverty and death.

Different environmental problems linked to the production and use of energy must be judged and choices made. A new coal plant in a poor country like Zambia will, on the one hand, increase carbon dioxide emissions but, on the other hand, will contribute to more food production and better functioning health clinics thereby saving thousands of lives.

You could argue that the Zambians should only use renewable energy. But in a world of limited resources where renewables still are a more expensive option than coal and other fossil fuels, which also means denying many poor people access to energy.

In a recent paper from the think tank Center for Global Development this choice was made clear. According to the report, $10 billion invested in burning gas for electrification could help lift 90 million people out of poverty. If the same amount was spent only on renewables, then it would merely help 20 to 27 million people, leaving more than 60 million in poverty and darkness and thousands to suffer an early death.

The British journalist Sebastian Mallaby tells a story about what can happen when we in the west try to impose a particular set of preferences (the result of our economic and cultural development) on poorer parts of the world. He learned from a Californian non-governmental organization that there were vigorous protests in Uganda against a large dam that the World Bank helped to finance near the source of the river Nile. The Ugandan environmentalist movement was supposedly up in arms against relocations and the environmental damage it would entail.

Mallaby went there only to find that the criticism came from a group of 25 members, funded by the Swedish Society for Nature Conservation (which in turn gets the money from Swedish development aid, i.e. from us taxpayers). When Mallaby spoke to people outside the 25 member group, every single one of them preferred electricity for clinics, schools and factories to the Swedish priority of unspoiled natural environment. According to Mallaby, the villagers happily accepted the payment to relocate, and the only people who objected to the dam were those living just outside the project's perimeter – they were angry since the project would not affect them, which meant that they would not get a generous payout.

There are no perfect solutions, only trade-offs, and they look different in different places - since the conditions differ and different things are at stake for different populations. What is hopeful is that all the options seem to be improving, because researchers are constantly giving us more knowledge and entrepreneurs are implementing new solutions. The costs of renewable sources are constantly coming down, safety at nuclear plants is improving, new dams are less destructive to aquatic life and the harm done by fossil fuels is being reduced by better methods of capturing the emissions.

Power to the People is a work in progress. The important question is how we can facilitate that work, and how we might damage it. That is a question to which we now turn.

v. Thomas L. Friedman, "The First Law of Petropolitics", Foreign Policy, April 25, 2006.

vi. "Oil Tanker Spill Statistics 2013", The International Tanker Owners Pollution Federation, London, 2014

vii. Andrew C. Revkin & Clifford Krauss, "Curbing Emissions by Sealing Gas Leaks", New York Times, October 14, 2009.

viii. "The fuel of the future", The Economist, April 6, 2013.

~ ~ ~

3. Picking Losers

"Politicians' Logic: Something must be done, this is something, therefore we must do it."

"Yes, Prime Minister"

There is always a temptation to try and solve the energy problem once and for all, with a top-down solution, where the government decides which way to go. It is a natural instinct when we face an overwhelming problem, and for politicians it is often done with good intentions. Politicians are well familiar with the problems of a reliable supply of energy and of the environmental costs, and when they think they have found a way forward - like solar energy - they want to promote it.

But giving public funds to particular projects is a way of replacing the knowledge, evaluations and market discipline supplied by thousands- even millions - of actors with the guesses of a small group of politicians and bureaucrats. "While that is good for us, I can't imagine it's a good way for the government to use taxpayer money," as one of the investors in the now defunct California solar company Solyndra described a very favorable government loan of $580 million dollars in 2009.

It also changes the company's priorities in a destructive way, from making customers happy to making politicians happy. One board member claimed that the hopeless company founder survived despite all his mistakes only because of his close relationship with the administration. Within a week of getting the first loan, Solyndra applied for another, worth $400 million.

Since the politicians and bureaucrats don't risk their own money, they don't devote the same time and energy to make sure that the investment pays off. One Management and Budget official complained that the Department of Energy's loan process had *"barely any review of materials submitted, no synthesis for program management and inherent conflicts in origination team members monitoring the deals they structured."*

Another temptation for picking winners is that politicians want to be seen doing something about problems. Just creating the right incentives and standing back might result in researchers and entrepreneurs coming up with better solutions, but it is not something for which politicians can take credit. If you have planned for something and subsidized something, you create particular jobs and photo-ops that wouldn't have been there otherwise.

Documents show that the White House wanted bureaucrats to rush their decision to grant Solyndra the huge loan so it could be announced on Vice President Biden's planned visit to California. As Biden put it when he announced the loan guarantee: *"these jobs are going to be permanent jobs. These are the jobs of the future."*

Suddenly it is all about appearance. Before president Obama's visit to Solyndra in May 2010, the administration famously asked an executive to lose the suit, another one to wear a hard hat and white smock and the workers to dress so that they created "the construction-worker feel."

And later on, when Solyndra had to lay off workers, a Solyndra adviser noted that the White House *"did push very hard for us to hold our announcement of the consolidation to employees and vendors to Nov. 3rd — oddly they didn't give a reason for that date."* November 2nd was the midterm elections of 2010. The day after, Solyndra announced that it would close its first factory

And, of course, politicians also get funding from the companies that benefit. That a wealthy Democratic fundraiser (through his family foundation) owned a third of Solyndra is not necessarily the reason for the subsidy, but it probably didn't hurt.

If none of these complicating circumstances had been present, even for a disinterested, rational, knowledgeable person, picking winners in the energy sector is at least as difficult as it is in other areas of the economy. It has often stuck us with the wrong solution at the cost of alternative solutions that could have worked better.

"Government is a crappy venture capitalist" as Lawrence Summers, then Obama's chief economic advisor, put it in relation to the Solyndra guarantee.

The premature rollout of nuclear power

No energy source is more closely associated with government

initiatives than nuclear power, and it shows both the benefits and the limitations of a top-down approach. In a way, it was a success of planning. In December 1953, President Eisenhower gave his "Atoms for Peace "speech before the United Nations. The nuclear bomb had shown the world destruction on an unprecedented scale, but it had also resulted in knowledge that could improve the world. Eisenhower now called on the world's nations to develop nuclear energy.

In those days five-year plans were not just for the Soviet Union. In 1954, the Atomic Energy Commission (AEC) announced a five-year plan where the government would develop this non-existent technology to give America world leadership. The first step was to find out which reactor design held the most promise. The results showed that only light water plants could be scaled up in a short time, partly because the design was developed for the Nautilus submarine reactor.

The design proved itself in December 1957 at the first reactor, built in Shippingport, Pennsylvania. It was built by Westinghouse, but the federal government paid 90 percent of the cost. The government was partnering with private companies to build larger plants, and managed to increase the size from 60 megawatts to 330 megawatts in just ten years.

The utility industry was not interested however, since fossil fuels seemed like a cheaper, safer bet than the constantly changing nuclear industry. But the reactor manufacturers, spurred on by government initiatives and subsidies, pressed on. In the early 1960's, Westinghouse and General Electric tried to awaken demand by constructing "turnkey" plants at fixed prices, where the utility only had to walk in, turn the key and start production. This resulted in many orders, and the great nuclear bandwagon effect of the 1960's. The AEC convinced utilities that prices were coming down rapidly and if manufacturers felt safe enough to promise them fixed costs it was also reassuring. So they ordered 49 reactors in 1966-67 at cost-plus contracts.

It was an amazingly quick rollout of an innovative technology, and it would never have been possible if it weren't for the government initiative and support. The only problem was that it wasn't necessarily the best technology. The utilities did not know it, but

Westinghouse and General Electric lost up to $1 billion on the turnkeys. And when they ordered reactors that were several times bigger than those in operation, they did not think of the complexities involved in a technology that was anything but routine.

Nuclear plant, Barsebäck, Sweden, now taken out of commission

Costs for the new plants were often underestimated by a factor of two, and long delays became common. Utilities lost millions and consumers got higher electricity bills in what James Cook in *Forbes* called "the largest managerial disaster in business history." Between 1978 and 1985, they cancelled 75 nuclear plants. Even before the Harrisburg accident, the first era of nuclear power was over.

When I talked to Dieter Helm, Professor of Energy Policy at the University of Oxford, about the future of energy, he pointed out that France made an even stronger bet on nuclear technology:

> *"In the 1970's people assumed that the oil and gas prices were going to go on ever upwards. France built 59 nuclear power stations on the basis of that. Almost all of them were out of the market for two decades. This is a risk we are running if politicians decide they know the answers, they know the winners and they're going to pick them."*

The American government thought it knew which technology would succeed and they could just pour the taxpayers' money into it to jump-start the future. The problem was that the light water reactor that was the closest to commercialization was not necessarily the best one long-term. But the government put all the eggs in the light water basket and so got the US – and the rest of the world - stuck in a particular technology that was unreliable and expensive. Since the government and the big manufacturers kept pushing a premature technology, the building and maintenance of the reactors never became a standardized routine business, which could have reduced both costs and safety hazards.

As pointed out by William Beaver, a professor of social science at Robert Morris University, who has written extensively on nuclear power, had it not been for the Cold War and the hunger for technological superiority, the government might have been satisfied with the first experimental stage, and then moved on to a slower and more cautious approach, where investments would have been based more on experience and demand, and less on political plans.

We might have seen a development of the other reactor designs, which were further from fruition in the early 1950's, and are only now beginning to reveal their potential:

> *"A government nuclear program more in line with the country's innovative traditions, without excessive government stimulation (roughly $7 billion in today's dollars by 1960), would have allowed the technology to become integrated into the American economic system. Decisions would have been made more on the basis of market conditions and less in response to political needs.*
>
> *Had this course been followed, General Electric, Westinghouse, and other manufacturers would have developed commercial reactors, but at a much slower pace. Nuclear power desperately needed time to mature. Consider that the last two 330-mw demonstration plants of the Power Reactors Program did not go on line until 1967, and by that time the manufacturers were taking orders for twice that capacity with little or no construction or operating experience. As Rickover told Congress when asked about scale-up, 'The minute you make a change in size you run into all sorts of problems'. In this regard, one Westinghouse official who headed the company's nuclear program at the time related that the entire industry needed a 'pause' to assimilate the experience gained by 1967 and to think about*

the future. Unfortunately, the rush to nuclear power was on and would not begin to slow for another decade. By that time, however, the damage had been done."

The unintended consequences of ethanol

Despite earlier failures, politicians often get carried away with new technologies that seem to promise energy in a better way, and they start promoting and funding them. For a time, it seemed like bioethanol would replace the expensive gasoline that fueled our cars. After all it's a fuel produced from agricultural feedstocks like sugar cane and corn and it seemed to make sense that we could grow our own fuel. In 2006, President George W. Bush declared that we were on our way to an "ethanol era" – "It's coming, and government can help."

The US government has subsidized it by more than $20 billion and required that all gasoline sold in the U.S. contain 10% ethanol. Many governments decided that ethanol was the fuel of the future so it was heavily subsidized. This would be the way to reduce CO_2 emissions while we help our corn farmers.

As so often happened before, it was a false start. A fifth of American cropland became dedicated to creating fuel, and many farmers switched from soybeans to corn, which resulted in much higher grain prices. This was great for corn farmers, but bad for other farmers, who use corn and soybean as inputs.

> *"It's hurt so much",* a dairy farmer in Pennsylvania tells me. *"My input costs have risen dramatically since all this. A couple years ago, a bushel of corn was $1.50. Last year it was $8.00. It's come down some since then. Soybean meal was $200.00 a ton just a few years ago. Right now we're paying $650.00 a ton for soybean meal to produce the milk from our cows. I think they've taken too much away from the food industry."*

In poor countries that were already suffering from food insecurity, the price rise had much more serious consequences. Experts and the United Nations warned that it was a way of taking food from the poor family's table, and putting it in the rich family's car. Higher prices also led to more global pressure on rain forests, which were converted into agricultural land.

Lynne Kiesling, Professor of Economics,
Northwestern University, Chicago

And absurdly, it soon turned out that ethanol didn't have the announced environmental benefits if you counted the energy it takes to plant, grow, harvest and process the crops and transport the ethanol. Lynne Kiesling, an economist at Northwestern University who specializes in energy issues, tells me that there have been unintended consequences:

> *"If you do an engineering lifecycle analysis of the production and the consumption of ethanol together, it turns out that the net energy effect is negative. The production of ethanol is an energy-intensive process, and it's not volumetrically equivalent to gasoline. For a given worth of energy out of the fuel, you need to use a little bit more ethanol versus gasoline. Once you put all that together, you're actually using energy by using ethanol more than you are saving energy. So it's not achieving that desired outcome.*
>
> *Another environmental aspect of ethanol is that it's very corrosive and has been very difficult to transport. Because of its particular physical properties, it would have to have its own pipeline network, which we don't have. You can't just put it in a natural gas pipeline, or a gasoline or an oil pipeline. So, how have we been shipping ethanol around the country? We do it by truck, which uses even more energy, and if there are spills it's also very problematic since ethanol is very*

hydrophilic and disperses very quickly into ground water.

So the unintended consequences of ethanol have been larger than anyone could've anticipated and overwhelmingly negative."

If ethanol doesn't make sense, why did the government promote it so heavily? Partly because the government believed in it. It's easy to make mistakes, and when you have access to tax money and regulation you can make very big mistakes. The decision was also heavily influenced by well-funded lobbyists, especially Archer Daniels Midland Corporation, which got much of the ethanol subsidy funding. So, a federal decision about exactly what fuel to promote, influenced by heavy special interest lobbying, has led to an agricultural and environmental negative and no real energy benefit.

What would have happened if governments didn't pick ethanol as a winner and promoted it heavily? Lynne Kiesling thinks it would have given us time to learn about the costs and benefits:

"I think experimentation with ethanol has been going on since the founding of the American Republic because we have such a large corn industry. In the absence of government intervention, that experimentation would have gone on, but in a smaller scale way and would be much more trial and error. We would have learned some of these physical properties and we would have learned about its energy cost and that it's really hydrophilic and corrosive.

We would have incurred some costs in that learning process, but it wouldn't have been this large spread of these costs across a whole lot of people, including international impacts on food prices. So I think one of the broader lessons that we could learn with respect to government trying to pick ethanol as a winner in the biofuel's market has been the amplification of those unintended consequences and the costs associated with them."

Renewables to the rescue?

Today we think we have learned from previous mistakes and politicians are not making the same ones again. Although they might abandon the hope that a particular energy source would be a winner, they are not giving up their belief that they are able to tell which the next one is.

Today governments all over the western world, but also in countries like China, are heavily promoting wind power, solar power and biomass. It would be an amazing accomplishment to satisfy our energy needs from the sun which just keeps on shining, or the wind which just keeps on blowing. It would be a natural, safe and clean source with no CO_2 emission.

A decade ago, European governments decided that Europe should lead the world on climate change. It would prove to the world that it was possible to de-carbonize the economy while at the same time develop new technologies, businesses and jobs. It would be a smart bet, because they assumed that the prices of oil and gas would just keep climbing. What looked like expensive renewables then would look cheap as fossil fuels doubled in price.

Copenhagen offshore windmills

Germany went further than any other country. After going back and forth on nuclear power for some time, the German government of Angela Merkel decided to abolish nuclear power after the Fukushima disaster in Japan in 2011 – suspiciously close to a few regional elections where she looked vulnerable, partly because the voters turned anti-nuclear. Germany has shut down eight nuclear plants so far.

At the same time the German government wanted to reduce the use of fossil fuels dramatically, like coal. It has been aggressively pushing renewables, like wind, solar and biomass, with the goal of obtaining 80 percent of electricity from clean energy by 2050. The German government has guaranteed producers of wind and solar energy a fixed high price for 20 years and given them preferred access on the electricity grid. It is called *Energiewende*, meaning"energy transition."

With the same fanfare that Eisenhower announced that nuclear was the future, and Bush declared an ethanol era, the German chancellor, Angela Merkel, talked about the bright, green German future:

> *"As the first big industrialized nation, we can achieve such a transformation toward efficient and renewable energies, with all the opportunities that brings for exports, developing new technologies and jobs."*

The goal was not just to solve a problem with energy supply and greenhouse gases, but also to become a world leader in a promising new technology. As the rest of the world also realized that these sectors were the future those companies would become global champions. We would see innovative European companies with European jobs.

The policy has succeeded in expanding the renewables sector dramatically. Its share of German electricity generation has increased from a tenth to more than 23 percent in ten years. Many countries have looked to Germany as a model.

But just like the initial problems associated with nuclear power, the problem was that the technology required for renewable energy was immature and staggeringly expensive. I have met many industry representatives who keep on telling me that just around the corner those sources will be competitive and even undercut fossil fuels. But if it were so, the question is why they constantly ask for more subsidies.

In 2013 alone the government subsidies cost Germans $26 billion to generate electricity with a market price of $3 billion. That cost is being passed on to consumers – partly because 2,300 companies with lots of lobbying muscle are exempted because they claim they couldn't handle international competition otherwise.

The then-Environment Minister, Jürgen Tritten from the Green Party, promised that the transition wasn't going to cost citizens more than one scoop of ice cream. But his successor, Peter Altmaier, was forced to admit that consumers are paying enough to "eat everything on the ice cream menu." The average German household now pays around $350 per year just to subsidize the renewables. Since 2000, electricity prices for households have increased 80 percent in real terms, and are around 50 percent higher than in other European countries.

"Electricity is becoming a luxury good in Germany," the German magazine *Der Spiegel* declares. More than 300,000 German households a year are seeing their power shut off because of unpaid bills. Caritas and other charity groups call it "energy poverty."

It is easy enough to measure the cost of a solar panel - (and it is coming down) and the capacity (and it is increasing). But there are other factors that decide how competitive it is and how much solar power costs. It depends on the cost of capital and how much of the time a plant operates. Therefore, we talk of *the levelized cost* – the net present value of all costs of building and operating a unit for its lifetime, divided by how many megawatt hours of electricity it produces.

This gives us an answer to the question of whether solar power is competitive in a place where the sun always shines. But that also means that the question gets more difficult. In most places, the sun doesn't always shine and the wind doesn't always blow. They can't be turned on and off. And, since there are no efficient ways of storing the energy, it's not always there when we need it the most. Whereas nuclear plants and natural gas plants run, on average, at around 90 percent of capacity, new wind farms run at around 25 percent of capacity, and solar only at 15 percent.

Trying to compare the costs and benefits of different energy sources is therefore a little bit like comparing apples with oranges that are not always available when we feel like eating an orange.

Charles Frank of the Brookings Institution has come up with a clever way of taking all these factors into account. He is looking not just at the capacity costs, but also at the costs that they avoid – costs that would have been incurred if the plant was not built. This takes into account the benefit of avoiding the coal that would have had to be burned if the renewables weren't there. It also accounts for the fact that a fossil-fuel plant must standby for when solar and wind does not deliver.

The upshot is that solar and wind is much more expensive than at first glance, due to very high capacity cost, very low capacity factors, and lack of reliability. According to Charles Frank, we have to invest around $10 million in wind power to produce the same amount of electricity with the same reliability as a $1 million investment in an efficient combined-cycle gas turbine. If we wanted to get the same solar capacity, we would have to invest no less than $29 million.

Nuclear plants can avoid almost four times more CO_2 per unit of capacity than wind power, and almost six times more than solar power. Highly efficient natural gas plants are as efficient as nuclear – they release much more CO_2 of course, but are much less expensive.

This implies a devastating problem for the whole green energy transition. By expanding the use of present day solar arrays and wind turbines, we have chosen the most expensive way of reducing greenhouse gases.

You could say that this is a cheap price to pay to accelerate innovation in, for example, solar. The ambition is not just to expand present technologies, but to speed up innovation as well. However, after a while, disappointed Germans realized that their companies were not becoming global champions at the hi-tech frontier. They slashed development departments to just produce and install solar panels en masse in order to take advantage of the subsidies.

The share of revenue budgeted for research and development shrank to 2 to 3 percent, compared to about 13 percent for innovative businesses like Microsoft and Google, the companies on which they wanted to model themselves.

And this isn't money going into blue-sky research or money being spent on trying to find a better way to harness the power of the sun. This is money which is going into the pockets of businesses, encouraging them to build and install the available technology.

Because they dealt with routine manufacturing, this made them vulnerable to competition, when Chinese companies started producing similar solar panels at a much lower cost. The only way to protect the European producers was to force tariffs on the Chinese, which the European Union did in 2013. They were lifted only when Chinese companies agreed to raise their prices and reduce the volume they export to Europe.

So in a perverse turnaround, a policy that was well intentioned to stimulate innovation and cheaper prices in solar power ended up reducing innovation and introducing protective tariffs against the cheapest alternatives.

Dieter Helm, Professor of Energy Policy and author of
The Carbon Crunch, University of Oxford, U.K.

Dieter Helm at the University of Oxford, has written critically about this transition in the book *The Carbon Crunch*. He tells me that he thinks Europe has got its priorities all wrong if it wants to combat global warming:

> *"What we've done is taken an early stage technology, the kind of solar panels we use at the moment and applied it on an enormous scale on the grounds that by applying it we'll get better at it.*
>
> *Now, the truth is, we have gotten better at it. But is that the real challenge over the next decades, getting better panels to strap onto peoples roofs? Or is it about opening up the light spectrum? Because solar uses a very, very small part of the potential energy that's available. Isn't it about developing new spray on solar films? Isn't it about thinking about using*

applications and materials in radically new ways?

Those sorts of improvements may not happen. But, one thing is pretty clear. They're not going to happen by getting better at strapping a solar panel onto your roof. Your panel will be better, but there's an order of magnitude question here. And it isn't the case we have infinite resource here. If you put all your eggs into that basket and spend enormous sums on doing it, there will not be sums of money available for the consumers and for other alternatives."

The Coal Question

When you start interfering with the market, you cause ripple effects throughout the system. When the sun doesn't shine and the wind doesn't blow, you need something to take its place. This could be nuclear power and natural gas, which are easy to switch on and off, but the Germans decided to abolish nuclear power. So, what about natural gas?

When you get renewables onto the existing system, you change the cost structure for everything. During the time of day when the wind does blow and the sun does shine, there is a lot of zero-marginal-cost electricity that forces everything else off the grid. This means that their intermittency renders natural gas intermittent as well. Since it now runs and gets any revenue only when renewables aren't available, it ruins the calculations behind the investment. It makes it economically impossible to invest in new gas plants.

What do the Germans have to turn to for backup capacity? Coal! The price of coal has plummeted and since nuclear was going offline, it suddenly seemed reasonable to keep the old coal plants open. Germany even decided to build 26 new coal plants. Since coal is much dirtier and emits almost twice as much carbon emissions as gas, the unintended consequence of the expensive Energiewende so far is actually an *increase* in the emission of greenhouse gases and increased pollution in German cities. In the rest of the European Union CO_2 emissions are being reduced, but in Germany, the country that would lead the transition, they have increased three years in a row.

This is the mother of all unintended consequences. It was supposed to be a green energy transition, but it takes even more coal than before to power it. Forty six percent of German electricity is now generated from coal. So the Germans dig more of it up – wherever it is - even lignite coal, some of the dirtiest coal in the world.

Dieter Helm is almost fascinated that Germany's politicians could get it so wrong:

"Like many people in the past they made the mistake. They assumed they knew where oil and gas prices were going to go.

The result is that Germany has an uncompetitive electricity price. It has a polluting energy sector. And it has no more security than it had in the first place. Indeed, in the absence of its nuclear power stations it has less security. It's not even protected itself from nuclear accidents since it's ringed with nuclear power stations in the neighboring countries. To have three objectives in energy policy: security, de-carbonization and competitiveness and to fail on one is something the politicians should answer for. But to fail on all three, that's a pretty big achievement."

On a beautiful day in May, this sad, ironic twist brought me to the beautiful, historic town of Atterwasch in Eastern Germany, close to the border with Poland. It is a small, picturesque town with some 250 people, surrounded by fields, forests and meadows. Many families here can track their family property back over centuries. Ancestors, parents and grandparents have lived on these same farms.

Father Matthias Berendt showed me the Lutheran Church, which was originally built in the 13th century. He didn't plan to stay there for long. He came from Berlin for his training and intended to go back. But he fell in love with the village and the people there, so he and his wife decided that he would accept a position there. *"Neighbors support each other, visit each other, are good friends and godparents for each other's children. A very nice place to live,"* Berendt says. He has lived here for 40 years.

Father Matthias Berendt, Atterwasch, Germany

But no more. Because the whole town of Atterwasch will be torn down. It sits on a rich vein of lignite coal. It is some of the dirtiet coal in the world, but it is necessary for Germany's energy transition. Germany's politicians have decided that the town has got to go and the people there will be forcefully removed.

Ulrich Schulz owns the largest farm in the village.

> *"I was born here," he says. "I grew up here. We've always lived here and made our living from agriculture and from the land, which my father, great-grandfather, great-great-grandfather managed and that is truly – not only to me, but to others as well – something special, that is no longer commonplace today.*
>
> *My father is 88 years old. When I talk with him, he avoids the topic. He says, 'I can't hear it, I don't want to hear it. I won't deal with it."*

Many of the villagers believed in the energy transition. They thought it would mean less fossil fuels and less coal. It seems like a sick joke that it resulted in more coal and more emissions and the end of their town. "That's the opposite of an energy transition," one villager tells me. "It's just idiotic."

A few minutes away by car is the huge brown coal strip mine, which will be expanded to swallow up Atterwasch and two other neighboring villages. It is a huge, dark hole in the ground, like something Saruman's armies would build in *The Lord of the Rings*.

Father Berendt tells me that their houses will be demolished, the corpses will be dug up and reburied, and the church will be blown up. All that will be left of the 800-year-old church will be a pile of rubble.

"It is like a death in the family," he tells me, with a sad look.

~ ~ ~

4. Outside the box, inside the rock

"The people who are crazy enough to think they can change the world, are the ones who do."

Steve Jobs

Jim Kennedy has seen good times and bad. His family lost all their cattle to the banks in 1943, the year he was born. He looks a bit like the archetypical rugged individualist, with a weather-beaten, sun-tanned look and a strong, calm manner. He sounds like it too, as he takes me around his land that he farms with two of his sons in Butler County, Pennsylvania.

> *"My first experiences of farming? If you don't do it, you don't get it done. You can't be successful. And I think that stands for about everything we do in life. You got to try it. You got to make sure that you're going to do it right and do your darndest to do it right.*
>
> *The best thing about farming is that I can make my own choices and live with my own choices, and that is also the challenge, because the decision you make today can affect you and your family for many, many years."*

Jim Kennedy

One of those choices has recently made Jim Kennedy a rich man. "You happen to be standing on it right now," he says and points to the ground, "but it's down there 9,000 feet." He is talking about the

Marcellus Shale, a gigantic shale rock with big natural gas reserves between the layers, reserves that are incredibly valuable. Less than a decade ago, land prices in the area were around $5 an acre. Today farmers can lease it out for extraction for $3,000-$4,000 an acre.

> *"It was an eye-opener for all of us. We didn't know it was there. And when we bought this farm, we didn't know it was there."*

But in fact, back when his great grandfather bought the property, no one thought that those reserves had any value, because there were no technologies to extract them. They didn't even exist 15 years ago. In the 1970's most people thought that the United States was running out of oil and gas. The big companies moved to foreign lands and offshore waters, and it was expensive and complicated. But one man was convinced that there must be some way to reach the domestic unconventional reserves.

George Mitchell was the son of a poor immigrant, who tended goats in Greece. He set up a shoeshine shop in Texas and the family lived above the shop. Mitchell himself worked throughout university and studied geology and petroleum engineering.

Eventually, he became a big player in the natural gas business in Texas, but he had a strange idea that set him apart from others. For a long time, companies had brought up oil and gas above and below the huge Barnett Shale, a thick layer of rock under Fort Worth. Mitchell, however, thought outside the box – inside the rock. He thought there must be some way to reach immense gas reserves inside the shale, thousands of square miles in area. This was considered absurd, since the only thing all engineers learned from the beginning was that you had to stay clear of the source rock.

So for 17 frustrating years Mitchell grappled with the rock, drilling hole after hole. His engineers and friends said that he was wasting his money. Some called him crazy. But he kept experimenting with new technologies and dropped by his company's engineering department every day to check on the development and pick new sites. He used hydraulic fracturing, fracking, which is a way of injecting high-pressure fluids into the ground to fracture the rock and create pathways for the trapped oil and gas. And he used a new method of drilling down and then sideways (horizontal drilling) to increase each well's yield.

Colleagues in the industry began to feel sorry for Mitchell, approaching his 80's. Some in the company talked of a miserable failure. But in 1997, Mitchell's team came up with the idea of replacing expensive foams and gels with a combination of water, sand and chemicals. This cut the costs radically and the company then began to combine it with horizontal drilling. This exposed thousands of feet of rock, rather than the 10 or 100 feet a vertical well reached.

The pieces suddenly came together, and the Barnett Shale was open. The goat-herders son could sell his company for $3.5 billion. No one called him crazy any more.

"That was the 'aha' moment," one person in the industry says. *"At that point, it was this worldwide breakthrough. At that point everyone was looking for the next Barnett."* And they all quickly learned how to use the right combination of fluids and horizontal drilling.

The United States suddenly experienced a natural gas revolution. By 2012, gas from shale accounted for about 35 percent of America's natural-gas production. Industrial gas prices were reduced by two-thirds between 2005-2012 (while they increased by 35 percent in Europe), saving consumers hundreds of billions of dollars a year. *The Economist* concluded that few businesspeople have done as much to change the world as George Mitchell.

The benefits of natural gas are obvious. It's abundant, it's cleaner, and it's cheaper. And it's in the United States, not in Russia or the Middle-East. The remaining technically recoverable resources could add another half century of natural gas reserves. Because of this, America has already surpassed Russia as the world's biggest producer of natural gas. Since many companies started using fracking to extract oil, some observers think it will even surpass Saudi Arabia as the biggest oil producer.

Natural gas is also a boon to the climate. Coal-fired plants are now being shut down all over the US as a result of the natural gas revolution. The US Energy Information Administration concludes that carbon-related emissions have been reduced by 12 percent since

2007. Some of this is the result of the recession, but the Administration specifically credits the increase in natural gas fired electricity generation.

Because of this development, in 2012, the United States became the first major industrialized economy to meet the United Nation's original Kyoto Protocol target for CO_2 reductions – even though the US never ratified it and wasn't bound by it.

The German government spent gargantuan sums in the energy sector with three goals in mind – security, de-carbonization and competitiveness – but failed on all three. The United States is right now getting much closer to all three goals, without really trying. Just by allowing people to experiment with their own local knowledge and giving them hope that they could gain remarkable fortune if they succeeded.

Lower energy prices might lead the way to a manufacturing renaissance. McKinsey Global Institute estimates that until 2020, shale gas and oil will add more than $500 billion to America's annual GDP, and create 1.7 million permanent jobs.

Because electricity prices are twice as high in Europe, no energy-intensive investments take place there now. In fact, many of them are contemplating relocating to the US. The German chemicals company BASF is allocating a quarter of its investment budget to the US. BASF is building a big propylene site on the Gulf Coast, which will use natural gas for both energy and as a raw material. The Austrian steel company Voestalpine is investing in a facility in Texas, where natural gas will be used as a fuel to make iron for Austrian plants.

Not so long ago, LNG (liquefied natural gas) ports were being built in the US to import natural gas. Now, those ports are being reengineered to export natural gas. Ten years ago, no one could see the United States as anything but a huge energy importer, but now it's on the verge of becoming one of the biggest exporters.

If the flow of oil were to be threatened in the future, perhaps because of events in the Middle East, America has a far better position than other countries- especially if natural gas also starts fueling cars and trucks.

In Lakeland, Florida, I visited Saddle Creek Logistics which operates warehousing and transportation capabilities for customers around the country. Their trucks might look much like any other truck, but as you get closer you see that they don't have the tall exhaust pipes other trucks have to get rid of dirty fumes.

Since 2012, Saddle Creek has begun to convert its fleet to CNG, Compressed Natural Gas. They noticed that the price of diesel was very volatile and wrecked their calculations, whereas natural gas prices were not just stable, but coming down. So far they have 200 vehicles that run on CNG and by 2015 they will have driven about 30 million miles on natural gas.

They have had to invest in new tractors with new engines and fuel tanks in addition to the development of new fueling and maintenance facilities. The challenge is that diesel holds a higher energy content per gallon, so natural gas needs a larger tank to get a reasonable operating range. But as the president, Mike DelBovo, shows me the fleet, it is fascinating to see how quickly they've come up with better models which are more aerodynamic and weigh less. In less than three years, Saddle Creek has come up with five different levels of trucks, and every generation goes further than the last one.

> *"It's better for the environment, it's better for fuel costs,"* Edward Hadley, a Driver Trainer at Saddle Creek, explains. *"And at the same time, I like it, because you don't go home smelling like diesel. Now my wife doesn't complain when she does laundry."*

The ecosystem that opened the shale

George Mitchell was the typical innovative entrepreneur, not just in imagination and persistence, but also in his eye for the discoveries of others. He didn't invent the technologies he used, but he found the right way to combine them and put them to a new, commercial use.

Mitchell also benefited from government investment in research. He had use for the geological surveys government agencies conducted, and hydraulic fracturing was helped along by Department of Energy research in the 1970's. The Carter administration implemented a tax credit for drilling for unconventional natural gas.

Before Mitchell, however, no one saw how you could combine all this information and these technologies to free natural gas from shale in a way that is economically competitive:

> *"In science, you have to be very aware of consensus," says Dan Steward, a former Mitchell Energy manager. "It's based on people's theories and models at the time. And sometimes it's damn wrong. And in this case it was damn wrong."*

The fracking revolution is the opposite of attempts to pick winners. When it came to nuclear, solar and wind, governments decided what they thought would win in the end. They planned for a transformed energy system and poured subsidies and privileges into the preferred sources.

The government was involved here as well - mostly by making sure there was knowledge and research available that others could use, and with a general tax credit that didn't pick preferred technologies. Government agencies could not even imagine how George Mitchell would use all of this. They thought he was crazy.

Picking winners is what happens when someone at the top decides what should work, and tries to get those below to adapt to it. Fracking was more the result of a spontaneous, bottom-up process where thousands of actors cooperated, competed and borrowed ideas from each other, so that technologies that seemed to work out in one context could be combined with other successful ideas and slowly float to the top.

Just look at the generations of innovation and entrepreneurship on which Mitchell's discovery depended. The slickwater mixture was used by Union Pacific Resources in East Texas before Mitchell used it. Hydraulic fracturing was pioneered in the 1940's by Stanolind Oil and Gas Corporation, a spin-off of Standard Oil. And, Halliburton created the first commercial wells. Horizontal drilling has a similarly complex background, dependent on a long series of inventions by entrepreneurs, going back to the 1930's. It is a story of modified gyroscopic compasses, landing survey tools, and rotary steerable systems. Before the use of downhole motors and precision tools to measure inclination, horizontal drillers would still have to stop constantly to make new surveys.

When George Mitchell started drilling, he could also make everyday use of an entire ecosystem of industries that invested commercially in equipment, collection and storage facilities, building rigs, drilling wells, constructing pipelines, and supplying all the energy it took to connect the sources to the markets. It also took an experienced labor force and deep capital markets to finance it.

It was also essential that it all happened on private property, that individuals owned the mineral rights and had the right to lease it to others. They were incentivized to let people work on their land, rather than trying to block the process at every stage.

The United States has more than 6,000 independent oil and gas companies and lots of associated service companies that are constantly competing with one another to come up with better solutions and serve their partners and customers even better. This amazing ecosystem of services that constantly evolves in response to new breakthroughs and changes in demand, is lacking when the government is trying to create a transition top-down. Then they can't take for granted that there is this market for all the surrounding services, where people try to help out with everything out of their own self-interest. The government has to plan to make all that happen as well, which is often much too complex a task.

This is also the reason why the shale gas revolution has not taken off in countries that have more top-down control of the energy sector. Most other countries only have a handful of big, bureaucratic companies in the sector and, if this system of services is not there, a single company can't do much. Since the mineral rights are controlled or owned by governments the landowners don't have an incentive to play along.

Some of the best shale reserves extend into Mexico, but so far they have hardly done anything to exploit it. And Europe and China, despite big reserves, are far, far behind. The founder of one fracking company estimates that around a thousand times more shale is now exposed inside the United States as outside it.

Controversies over fracking

Fracking is controversial and has its own sets of problems. Over the last few years many fears have been raised about the process. In a famous scene in the 2010 anti-fracking documentary GasLand they set fire to the water from the kitchen faucet, claiming that fracking had released methane.

This turned out not to be the case. Colorado officials investigated the claim and concluded that the homeowner had drilled his own water well into naturally occurring pockets of gas. But still, there are worries and real risks related to the use of chemicals and water. The risk of contamination of the groundwater has to be taken into consideration.

Lots of water and sand is being used in the process, and some chemicals used in the fracking process can be health risks if they're released at the surface. If drilling isn't done properly, chemicals or natural gas could be released into groundwater. In one case in Pennsylvania, the borehole had not been properly cemented so some methane migrated to surface water and the company had to return and add cement.

There are no perfect solutions - all energy sources have their problems, costs and benefits. If we rule out something because it's not perfect, we might end up with something that is worse. The energy expert Dieter Helm at Oxford University, agrees that fracking has serious environmental problems, but he adds:

> *"So does coal mining. So does oil extraction. So do all fossil fuels. If you're a country like Germany or France and you go around banning fracking, do remember what the alternative you are pursuing is. So I find it stunning that a country like Germany could expand lignite and coal burn and production and ban fracking.*

> *Let's remember what fracking looks like lined up against coal mining. Coal mines are almost always in the water table. They leach heavy metal. They belch out methane on an enormous scale. They are energy intensive in their own right. They damage the health of every single person who goes anywhere near a coal mine. They kill a lot of people. And that's before you take the coal and take it to the power station and produce SOx, NOx, carbon emissions, and before you use a lot of water to cool the power station and then get rid of the ash afterwards.*

If you want to ban fracking then you must make it a criminal offense to dig coal."

Since all of us suffer from a fear of the new and unfamiliar, it's important to put the problems of fracking into context, and compare it to what we are already doing. The investor Ron Muhlenkamp is a landowner and an environmentalist who lives above the Marcellus Shale and wanted to find out what was going on in his backyard. While doing the research he found that much of the fear was overblown and he has come up with several enlightening comparisons.

It takes around five million gallons of water to drill a typical well and to fracture the shale that drains the gas from underneath 80 acres. That is a lot of water. But Muhlenkamp also points out that it is the equivalent of 2.3 inches of rain over those 80 acres, where the annual rainfall is 35-40 inches. We can also compare it to the water usage in other forms of energy production, which few complain of being excessive. In terms of the energy output, shale gas is 14,000 times more water efficient than corn ethanol, for example.

New treatment technologies also make it possible to recycle water recovered from the fracturing. And of course, water is also a byproduct of burning natural gas, and can be recovered.

Muhlenkamp recognizes that chemicals make up 0.5 percent of the fluids used for fracking, but points out that these are the same chemicals that we put in swimming pool cleaners, candy, toothpaste, detergents, soap and cosmetics. The point is not to mock health hazards, but to point out that toxicity is not an absolute. Toxicity always depends on the concentration. The need is to handle them in the right way and take care of them correctly. We wash the dishes we eat from with toxic chemicals, so we must rinse them well.

Sometimes this does not happen. There are examples of reckless drilling and usage of chemicals. Early on drillers used to just pour concrete into the gap between the well casings and the surrounding earth, letting gravity take care of the rest, which allowed for some voids in the concrete. Now they are pumping the concrete down the casing, which results in a better seal.

George Mitchell himself thought that fracking had to be carefully regulated. He warned about less experienced frackers cutting corners, which would harm both the environment and the technology's reputation. It is important to make sure that they don't drill close to water tables, that the chemicals and water usage is controlled, and that methods to capture the methane leakage are used.

But many of the questions on whether or not to frack, and how to do it, do not have one simple answer. There are difficult questions, and it's not certain that the trade-offs look the same everywhere. Lynne Kiesling, the energy economist, thinks that this is an argument for putting many of the decisions into the hands of those that are most affected. One size doesn't always fit all, she says:

> *"These are real and important questions and this conversation is going on at the local level in a lot of these communities, and I think that's where it should be happening, because it uses local knowledge, and it harnesses the potential for community self-governance to determine what activities are done there.*
>
> *Folks in the community have the local knowledge. They know what is at stake for them, what they are willing to do, how important the jobs are that are associated with the industry, and how they weigh costs and benefits.*
>
> *If you implement things like water quality benchmarking before the drilling starts, so that you have very, very clear guidelines for the drillers they'll be able better to identify whether or not they have actually produced any contamination. And then you've got very clear legal means for assessing penalties.*
>
> *And to the extent that there is some commonality across what communities are experiencing, there's a role for information sharing of best practices and facilitating the sharing of best practices."*

Jim Kennedy, the Pennsylvanian farmer, is certain about his choice, because he knows that the drillers want to leave behind a happy landowner (and no lawsuits). To transport the gas they had to build a pipeline, but it is buried eight feet deep in most places and covered so they can farm over it. Drilling is noisy, but once it is drilled it just sits there for 25-50 years, pumping gas. First they drill down 9,000 feet and then they go 6,000 more feet lateral. So Kennedy challenges my assumption that it will disturb him:

> *"Have you felt anything today? If you haven't felt anything today, then you know how we all feel. It is like this, peaceful, quiet. It's down there. It's not going to be bothersome.*
>
> *We all need clean drinking water. It's a life resource for all of us. But it's well below the water table, which is only down around 6-800 feet, and encased in concrete. A leak into the water table is not going to happen.*
>
> *The chemicals themselves are very closely regulated. The Department of Environmental Protection is here all the time. There isn't a day that there isn't environmental inspectors here to make sure everything is handled correctly. Everything around a well site is contained. It's got a barrier around it. It cannot get away. It is taken and disposed of properly."*

When I listen to Jim Kennedy and his enthusiasm for the project I think back to the farmers and villagers in Atterwasch, Germany, who despaired about how they would be forced off the land of their ancestors to dig for coal. It's difficult to imagine a sharper contrast between negotiated local solutions - based on property rights and freedom of agreement - and a top-down command solution.

In the end, Kennedy gives a strong argument for the case that these decisions have to be taken locally, because no one cares more about the land and its future than the farmers:

> *"We should be concerned, because you don't want somebody in there doing a job that would hurt future generations. You know once the well drillers are gone and once the pipeline people are gone, we're still here. We farmers are still here, and we want to make sure our land continues in production, and that's why we've got to make sure that we spell out contracts the way we want them."*

~ ~ ~

5. Powering the future

"If you want to have good ideas you must have many ideas. Most of them will be wrong, and what you have to learn is which ones to throw away."

Linus Pauling

"The problem with the environmentalist movement is that it's utopian. It wants perfection. And there is no such thing in any human endeavor." The policy analyst Shikha Dalmia argues that environmentalists must learn to accept trade-offs if they want to save the world:

> *"It keeps waiting for that perfect energy technology that requires no tradeoffs – no carbon emissions, no sulfur dioxide emissions, no smog, no particulate matter. And of course, there is no such thing as a perfect energy source out there.*
>
> *The rational way for the environmental movement to think about it would be: compared to what? If we are incrementally moving energy in a more environmentally sustainable and cleaner direction, that ought to be a good thing, but that's not how the movement thinks about it. So, with fracking and natural gas, even though it'll cut carbon emissions, even though we know it's a very clean form of energy, it is not good enough for the environmental movement."*

Since so much is at stake, for mankind and for the environment, it is tempting to go looking for that one, best solution to the energy problem. But, the conclusion of my investigation, my travels and all the discussion I've had on the subject is that we must avoid that, precisely because so much is at stake. The simple and surprising - and for many people disappointing - answer is that there isn't just one best source. What's "best" changes with where you live and it changes over time.

"There are no silver bullets. Everything has tradeoffs, and there are no easy answers," Lynne Kiesling puts it. The technologist and science writer Ramez Naam agrees: *"There is no energy source that is perfect. Every energy source has a negative or at least a limitation. There's no such thing as the perfect Holy Grail of energy."*

"Think about it this way," Dieter Helm says, "if ministers could really pick the right energy technologies, we should all be socialist planned economies like the Soviet Union because if they know how to decarbonize, then why don't they know better how to make aluminum or boots or cars? I mean, this is nothing more than the general argument that leaving private individuals and private firms to seek out efficient ways of doing something is almost always better than the travesties of state planning that we witnessed in the 20th century."

Governments have tried to solve this problem for a long time, and enormous resources have been used to do so. The result is not encouraging. There is no stronger contrast than how Germany tried to change the entire energy system from the top, and how the US government stepped back and allowed entrepreneurs to search for different solutions. And the outcome is obvious. Germany ruined its competitiveness with higher electricity prices It had to protect it's failing companies with tariffs while simultaneously burning more coal and increasing CO_2 emissions On the other hand, the US reduced prices, built new, strong companies and reduced CO_2 emissions.

So, it seems to me that the world needs fewer top-down planners, and more crazy dreamers like George Mitchell - people who are venturing into new territory and exploring strange new ideas. We need more people who experiment with new technologies and solutions, and if they stray far off the consensus that's only to be welcomed, because it means that we investigate more possibilities and get knowledge that others are not looking for. Most of these experiments will be failures, but it only takes a few to change the world.

A work in progress

In fact, scientists and entrepreneurs are right now hard at work trying to improve on old technologies, inventing new ones and finding completely new roads ahead. In the sectors where governments tried to kick-start technologies, nuclear, ethanol and solar (often only to reach dead ends) the slow but steady progress of knowledge accumulation and experiments now show promise. Let's take another look at them.

The nuclear reactors that are supplying the United States – and Sweden – with electricity are so called Generation II nuclear - the ones that the American government promoted aggressively and that took over the market completely. However, since then we have seen the step-by-step improvement in design, based on experience and new knowledge which should have taken place from the start. Generation III reactors have better thermal efficiency, superior fuel technology and passive safety systems that rely on physical phenomena. The improved safety and reduced costs have extended the operational life of reactors by about a third.

The Fukushima Daiichi disaster was a result of a power loss that made it impossible to cool the radioactive fuel and spent fuel. A passive safety system would have used nothing but gravity to circulate water in order to cool down the plant in an emergency and circulated cool outside air.

Right now, scientists and companies are working on Generation IV nuclear power. So far, it is a summary term of reactors that are only experimental. They are all passive safe, get hundreds of times more energy from the same fuel and don't have the same problems with waste. Fast reactors can burn the waste as well. One safety aspect is that a fast reactor burns liquid metal fuels. When they overheat, the fuels expand and that in itself slows down the reaction. A Chernobyl or Harrisburg disaster would not be possible.

The real game changer would be the small, modular reactors that some companies are working on. Bill Gates has invested in TerraPower. The company's goal is to build a traveling wave reactor that uses radioactive waste as a fuel, doesn't have to be refueled and cannot melt down. The idea is to have them built in factories, completely sealed and able to run for several decades without any human intervention. The reactor could also serve as the unit's burial cask. If this worked, they could just be dropped into a concrete hole – "build, bury, and forget." TerraPower's founder is hopeful:

> *"We could power the world for the next one thousand years just burning and disposing of the depleted uranium and spent fuel rods in today's stockpiles."*

Even though ethanol in the version the government subsidized was a complete failure, we now see exciting developments in bio-fuels as well. Big companies like ExxonMobil and Chevron, as well as small, innovative startups are working on how to develop a new generation of biofuels – from algae.

It can produce 30 times more energy per acre than traditional ethanol, and the goal is to modify it to produce hundreds of times more energy. But that is not the only advantage. It can be grown anywhere so it doesn't have to compete with valuable farmland, and can use seawater instead of freshwater. Since algae feed on CO_2, we could turn the smokestacks around and feed the algae emissions we don't want in the atmosphere.

> *"The end of the oil age will come when we have some renewable replacement for oil", Ramez Naam says. "If we get something like algae bio-fuels where you can just turn land and sunlight into gasoline, that's when it'll come. There are some very exciting companies that are working on this, but the history of bio-fuels is littered with the dead corpses of companies that have not been able to move from their demonstration scale to the scale where you can really affect the market.*
>
> *But the science says it's possible. It's possible to turn sunlight and water and carbon dioxide in the atmosphere into gasoline. That's what plants and pressure and refineries do. We should be able to do it but we haven't figured out the engineering to do it at scale yet. Someday someone will, and that person will make a fortune and do a huge value for the planet."*

There are also fascinating new possibilities that might help us get our energy from the sun. Graphene is an incredible new material that was produced for the first time in 2004, at the University of Manchester. It is an unbelievably thin and flexible sheet, just one carbon atom thick, which makes it almost two-dimensional. At the same time it is remarkably strong, doesn't corrode and conducts heat and electricity efficiently. This could drastically change the economics of solar power. Most solar cells today use expensive indium, whereas carbon atoms are not exactly rare.

So far, graphene is not very good at collecting the electrical current from inside the solar cells, but scientists are hard at work trying to solve that problem. If they do, perhaps we could turn anything into a solar power station in the future. Imagine if your house, your car or even your clothes were covered in solar film.

But until we are there, we have to learn to live without a Holy Grail. It would be counterproductive to block any alternative because it is not perfect. Nuclear power has its problems, but it's too important a large-scale non-fossil fuel to reject it. The green pioneer Stewart Brand recently pointed out that environmentalists have caused gigatons of carbon dioxide to enter the atmosphere because they blocked nuclear power: He confesses, *"I was part of that too, and I apologize."*

Natural gas is also problematic, but it is a cheap energy source that is less harmful to the climate than other fossil fuels. It could provide us with a bridge to a future with even better, cleaner energy sources.

Perhaps we should abolish nuclear power and avoid hydraulic fracking for natural gas, but not before we have abolished every coal plant on the planet. Even coal has a role to play as long as better alternatives are not available in a cheap and efficient way. The worst alternative is not coal, but life without access to electricity.

The author at strip mine near Atterwasch, Germany

In laboratories around the world, tens of thousands of scientists and engineers are trying to revolutionize energy – from making our everyday appliances intelligent, to colonizing space. If just one of them is successful, it will blow our minds and change the world.

Some are dreaming of solar power in space, where there is no night and no atmospheric gases or clouds to block the sun. Some sort of microwave transmitter or laser emitter would direct energy to the areas of earth that need it for the moment. But we would probably need big breakthroughs in telerobotics to build and maintain solar panels in space.

Closer to home, others are working on an internet for energy – an intelligent and decentralized network of power lines, sensors and switches where both producers and consumers can put information and power into the network - and take it out. This could lead to appliances shutting themselves off when they are not needed or when energy is scarce, so the dishwasher starts in the middle of the night instead. It might also be a way of dealing with the storage problem, since energy that is not used can be stored in appliances, cars and homes. You could charge your car when electricity prices are low and send it back to the grid when prices are high.

Many companies are working on artificial photosynthesis, where no organism is needed to turn sun, water and CO_2 into "solar fuels." As I write this, one German company just opened a facility where they turn 3.2 tons of CO_2 into 160 gallons of fuel every day. Others are genetically modifying bacteria to make them eat waste and excrete crude oil.

The famous geneticist Craig Venter is experimenting with designer algae. You decide whether you want gasoline, diesel or jet fuel, and then just give the algae the right DNA instructions.

Several scientists are working on ways of removing CO_2 from the air. It might sound far-fetched but, after all, this is what trees do every day. We can do it. So far, the projects seem incredibly expensive, but technologies change. It would be a way of not just reducing, but actually reversing global warming. A great benefit would be that the machines could be placed anywhere. They don't have to be close to the source, so they can be placed where energy is the cheapest and where it is easy to store and make use of the carbon dioxide.

Some even dream of using strong lasers, precise radio waves and the earth's natural magnetic fields to push the CO_2 emissions out of the atmosphere and into space. Even if it that technology works, it will come with great risks and unintended consequences. What if we got rid of too much CO_2 - what would cool the earth? Risks like that are also involved in another form of geo-engineering that Ramez Naam tells me about:

> *"We could reflect some of the sun's energy back into space. We know about this because of a volcanic eruption that occurred that lowered the earth's temperature by about one degree Celsius for a couple years. This happened because it injected aerosols, sulfur molecules into the stratosphere and those are small and shiny and reflected the sun just a little bit – less than a percent, less than 1/1,000th actually of the sun's energy back into space. And that was enough to drop the earth's temperature by that much.*
>
> *Could we do that ourselves? Could we fly planes or have balloons at very high altitude in the stratosphere, 80,000 feet up, to pump up these aerosols and reflect some of this energy back in to space? People want to try this. And there's a decent chance it would work. And if it did work it would be relatively cheap, meaning it might cost millions or tens of millions of dollars which is not very much compared to billions or trillions. But, it wouldn't stop other problems related to carbon dioxide, like the acidification of the oceans that might eventually kill off half the sea life there. And it would do other things as well, like changing rainfall patterns around the globe, which might have consequences as severe as climate change since agriculture depends on that.*
>
> *So, we should definitely do more research in to it, but it's not ready for prime time yet."*

Having this preparation might be a useful insurance policy. If the worst global warming scenarios were to play out, it might be worth taking risks.

There are so many fascinating projects out there. Some might sound crazy, but that is what everybody thought of George Mitchell as well. We need all those experiments, because I don't know what will work out in the end, and you don't know. And we have learned that the government certainly doesn't know.

Ramez Naam, futurist and writer

The role of government

The government *can* help out, in two ways. First of all it can fund basic research to increase our collective knowledge. In the first step of the American nuclear power project it did help development along by collecting knowledge and results on an untested new power source and sharing it with others. It was only when the government tried to kick-start the process and chose particular technologies that it became problematic.

The problem, again, is that it is so tempting for politicians to pick winners and subsidize particular companies, resulting in massive grants to present technologies - not helping us to move on. It might even hold back progress, since limited resources might be directed to the wrong technology. If we spend them all on present technologies there are less resources for the new ones.

Europe uses hundreds of billions of dollars annually to subsidize the present generation of renewable energy sources, but they can't find 125 million dollars to fund research in graphene. A small development in graphene research would be worth thousands of wind farms and millions of solar panels.

The other thing that most of the experts I talk to agree upon is that the government has to deal with the problem of externalities. If we pay for the damage we do, we have to take into account the environmental costs involved in energy production.

> *"Because I cause that cost, I should pay a price in the way I pay a price for any other cost I impose,"* Dieter Helm says. *"And if I have to pay a price for my pollution, I'm going to take into account how I do stuff. So, if I use energy that's carbon intensive, it'll be more expensive. If I use nuclear energy, it will be a lot cheaper because I start to substitute."*

Ramez Naam argues for a carbon tax:

> *"I think a revenue-neutral carbon tax is the simplest and fairest way. No, exemptions, no special carve outs, it's just every ton of carbon emitted costs X dollars, let's say it starts at zero and goes to a hundred dollars.*
>
> *And, all of that money raised is used to reduce the payroll tax from the bottom up and, when that's gone, the income tax from the bottom up. Starting with the poorest people because they face the most. That means that people have more money in their pocket to pay their energy bills and it's totally neutral and totally fair."*

This means that the government provides an incentive, but it doesn't tell us what to do. It wouldn't pick winners, it wouldn't subsidize the energy sources it prefers nor limit how we can consume energy.

It wouldn't tell us how to de-carbonize, it would leave it to millions of consumers and businesses to find the most efficient and cheapest way to minimize the carbon cost. Someone might use less energy. Someone else might change from coal to natural gas. The market will be looking for better solutions all the time, supply and demand solutions that no centralized bureaucracy can even know about. As Helm puts it:

> *"It's almost certainly going to do it more efficiently than some bureaucrat in some government office is going to do it. In the market, reality is reality. You pay the cost. You're not there to be lobbied. You're not there because you got subsidies. You know that if you get it wrong, you pay."*

A realistic strategy for our energy future also has to take into account the global character of climate change. Today, there is no effective way to curb carbon dioxide emissions world-wide, at least not to the degree required to have a noticeable effect on predicted future climate change. Presently, there are no signs that such a universal system of governance is achievable - quite the contrary. It is obvious that the governments now presiding over rapidly developing economies are disinclined, to put it mildly, to any multilateral agreement on climate change that would actually make a difference.

The curious multilateral dance around climate issues in the last few years says something about how hopeless it seems to wait for action from the government. The first international climate assembly took place in 1995, but the countries could only agree on a deal after the third meeting in Kyoto 1997. This did not cover the most important countries, China and the US, but European leaders claimed that others would decide to catch up if Europe only moved ahead.

But nothing much happened until expectations grew ahead of the Copenhagen meeting in 2009, partly because Obama was newly elected as US president. However, this meeting ended in a collapse, and China and the US made a separate deal without commitments. At the meetings in Cancun and Durban the intention was to extend Kyoto but, instead, big signatories like Japan, Russia and Canada began to give up on a deal. Instead of leading the way, Europe was becoming isolated. The only result was an agreement to try to reach an agreement about an objective. Almost two decades after Kyoto, the world community has agreed to try to agree in 2015 on what they should agree upon in 2020.

Countries still struggling with feeding their population and getting their kids into schools will not be convinced by any kind of rhetoric from rich countries responsible for putting most of the CO_2 in the atmosphere to begin with. They will not restrain themselves or switch to other energy sources because we tell them that something else is better. In fact, in most instances, they don't even know where all the sources of pollution are within their countries.

The only way to get countries to switch to greener alternatives is if those alternatives are also competitive economically. If we can offer better technologies that use less energy and less expensive ways of producing electricity and fuel, those technologies will spread over the world spontaneously.

The Ultimate Resource

I don't know where the next big idea is going to come from. We don't know which technology might help us to power the world. But, what makes me an optimist is that tens of thousands of scientists and entrepreneurs are right now hard at work trying to develop brand-new energy sources and to perfect amazing technologies, because they think they know the answer. And they are working hard to prove it - to save the world and make a fortune in the process. They think they know, and at least one of them is probably right.

We can get through this. We may be destructive as a race, but we are also incredibly inventive. If there is anything that we've learned from the fracking revolution, it is that we will be surprised by new technological breakthroughs in the future. It is heartening to hear that the experts I meet are all, to some degree, optimistic about our future despite all the problems we face – poverty, lack of energy, environmental problems and counterproductive policies. *"I have faith in humanity. I have faith in human ingenuity,"* Shikha Dalmia concludes her interview.

Ramez Naam shares this faith:

> *"I think we can overcome all of the issues facing us. I think we can save the planet and keep growing that pie and making ourselves richer. I think we can solve poverty and still make the planet better off by innovating, by creating new ideas, new technologies, new scientific breakthroughs that allow us to get more energy, more food, more water with less damage done to the planet and that's the way to lift billions out of poverty while at the same time solving climate change."*

Dieter Helm again:

> *"In my lifetime, I have never known so much research taking place. Every bright student wants to do energy now. There are ideas coming out on all the dimensions of the energy sector which could easily be as transformative as what happened in my lifetime in IT with the development of web*

THE REJUVENATION TRILOGY BOOK THREE

REJUVENATION 3

Out of a clear, blue sky a mysterious alien race wreaked havoc on planet Earth, thus beginning the Melter War.

Alien energy weapons struck the Polar ice caps. Oceans rose, drowned huge swathes of land, swallowed up great cities and left much of the earth as an irradiated wasteland.

Millions of people died.

But a savior emerged; Lisette Fox and her Belus Corporation supplied the weapons and technology to defeat the Melters and brought peace back to the world.

Some two decades later Bobbie Chan, a child at the outbreak of war, now works as a doctor caring for the ultra-elderly. Bobbie encounters a previously unidentified disease; 'Rejuvenation' which makes the old young but has homicidal side effects.

In this gripping final instalment of Byddi Lee's Rejuvenation trilogy Bobbie discovers the shocking truth behind the Melter's attack and Rejuvenation. Bobbie faces a decision with untold consequences, not only for Bobbie, but for the entire human race.

BYDDI LEE IS AN IRISH writer living back in her hometown of Armagh, after having lived abroad for many years. Before she wrote "Rejuvenation", a speculative fiction trilogy, published by Castrum Press, she had success publishing flash fiction, short stories and her novel, "March to November". Byddi co-founded and manages Flash Fiction Armagh, shortlisted as Best Regular Spoken Word Night in the Saboteur Awards. She co-edits "The Bramley – An Anthology of Flash Fiction Armagh".

Along with two other members of the Armagh Theatre Group, Byddi wrote: "IMPACT – Armagh's Train Disaster" which was staged, for the anniversary of the fragedy, in June 2019 in the Abbey Lane Theatre in Armagh and "Zoomeo & Juliet" a live play performed on Zoom, by the Armagh Theatre, during the 2020 UK-wide COVID-19 Pandemic lockdown.

ISBN 9780990769576

90000

9 780990 769576

and mobile phones and so on.

And just think about it, the new materials like graphene, the ability to think of next generation solar, the fact that we may learn how to store energy. The idea that transport may switch from oil base to electricity base. The idea that we might use information technology to move from a dumb and passive demand side to active management of our energy usage, all of those things are transformational, each in their own right, but the package of them together leads me to think that it's much more promising than all those ghastly political "2050 roadmaps" and plans.

By 2030 the energy world may look dramatically different. And it's not utopian to imagine that we may have technologies which lead us to leave quite a lot of those fossil fuels in the ground not because we decided to do that, but because there are cheaper and better alternatives which are more competitive."

Lynne Kiesling:

"I am an optimist, because I think that it is human nature to strive and to seek new ideas, come up with better ways of doing things, and that we are boundlessly creative. Economist Julian Simon talked about human beings as the ultimate resource. The ultimate resource is that we are boundlessly creative. We are always applying our creativity to come up with new and better ways to do things, and that's not going to change."

The human brain is the resource that just keeps giving. It discovers and creates new resources and new ways of using the old ones. The increase in energy use is facilitating education and connectivity, so that this ultimate resource is becoming even more productive and valuable.

Since the 1950's the global illiteracy rate has been reduced from 50 percent to less than 20 percent. All those literate individuals now have access to the knowledge and talent of others in an unprecedented way. Almost three billion people have access to the internet - two billion people have it in their pocket. With just one

Google search they use more computing power than the whole Apollo project used in the eleven-year mission to put a man on the moon. The Chinese bought 100 smartphones in just the last three months. A population that was completely isolated from the rest of the world suddenly has access to the world's reservoir of knowledge on their phones.

Children walking home from school in Issidan Izdar, Morocco

In an open world, new ideas and technologies can be created anywhere in the system, not just in the center. In the last few years we have seen a surge in innovations and business models from unexpected places, often from young people, who have built new solutions on top of what they have learned on the web. Perhaps that is where we should expect the next surprising breakthrough in energy, in materials or storage.

When the Massachusetts Institute of Technology gave its first online course, 150,000 students signed up. It was a course in Circuits and Electronics, which required some advanced mathematics. Not even every 400th student got a perfect score. One of them was a 15-year old from Ulan Bator in Mongolia, who didn't even read English well.

Battushig Myanganbayar took the course because he thought it would help him understand how a smartphone worked, and he got hooked. He didn't read much of the literature, since he didn't really understand the language. Instead, he spent a lot of time surfing the web to learn about the differential equations and other things he needed to keep up with the course.

After a while, he started making short films on his mobile phone that taught other young Mongolians how they could understand the course. MIT even recruited him to improve their online courses. In an electrified, connected world, it is easier for knowledge and technology to reach the talented wherever they hide. And, it's easier than ever for them to put their ideas and their hard work at the world's disposal.

As the spread of electricity makes more people connected, more people learn about what is going on and they get the tools to participate. The problem that everybody is talking about – our thirst for energy – is also the solution to the problem.

This month, a 12-year old girl in a small Moroccan village got access to electricity for the first time, and she takes her first steps online. She is about to enter a global world. She has access to the sum of mankind's knowledge, and can add her own ingenuity to it.

Our challenges are huge, but we also have more eyeballs looking at them than ever. And, more brains than ever are trying to come up with innovative solutions.

~ ~ ~

About Johan Norberg

Johan Norberg is an analyst and writer from Sweden. He focuses on globalization, entrepreneurship, and individual liberty. He is a senior fellow at the Cato Institute and author and editor of several books exploring the global economy and its challenges, including his most recent book, *Financial Fiasco: How America's Infatuation with Homeownership and Easy Money Created the Economic Crisis.* His landmark book, *In Defense of Global Capitalism,* was originally published in Swedish in 2001, and has since been published in over twenty different countries. In recent years Norberg has been the presenter and narrator of several public television programs in the United States produced by the Free To Choose Media. He has been active in the writing and production of these programs including "Free or Equal," "Europe's Debt, America's Crisis," "Power to the People," and the upcoming "World of Adam Smith."

Norberg's articles and opinion pieces appear regularly in both Swedish and international newspapers, and he is a regular commentator and contributor on television and radio around the world. For his work he has received several awards, including the Sir Antony Fisher Memorial Award and the gold medal from the German Hayek Stiftung. His personal website is http://www.johannorberg.net/

~ ~ ~

Credits

Photo credit: Resolution Productions, Inc.

Cover design credit: Len Juniewicz and Robert Range

~ ~ ~

Printed in Great Britain
by Amazon

58478612R00054